REUNITED

When the Past Becomes a Present

A *Love* Story

ANN VOTTA

For Our Children: Steve, Joey, Cheryl, David and Leigh

And for my mother, Helen Patavino, who has always pointed me in the right direction.

Acknowledgements

*F*IRST OF ALL I want to thank God for bringing Alan and I together again. And secondly I wish to thank Alan for making me so happy in the life we now share with one another. After all—that's what our story is all about. And this wouldn't be a story without Alan's daughter-in-law, Catherine Votta, encouraging him to go on Facebook. We are eternally grateful to her for her inspiration.

And we both thank all of our children for making us so proud of who they are and in everything they do.

Special thanks go to my daughter, Leigh Vincola (an accomplished writer herself), who was the only person to read the very first draft. She helped enormously in structuring the book and offering initial suggestions and encouragement to keep me going. She has also read several editions of the manuscript, continuing to edit and offering critical overview at each juncture.

I also wish to thank the friends and family who read a draft of the manuscript rather early on which helped set the stage of what would come—Sis (Anne Mateer), Teenie (Adrienne Votta Hochberg), and Pam Kerns. They spurred me on by providing insight and praise. Other helpful readers were Kathy Grabowski, Brianne Matter, Tammy Stroupe and Joseph Gianguzzo.

Special thanks also go to Nicole Bokat, my editor, who provided professional detail and information about publishing in general, as well as offering much encouragement and support.

But most important is the assistance and love that Alan has given me throughout the project. We have spent thousands of hours reading, re-reading, editing and embellishing our story. Without his help I really couldn't have accomplished this. And his sense of pride in what I have done in completing the book has overwhelmed me. It has been a joint effort of immense proportion. So often we would find ourselves in tears, crying over something lovely that happened as we re-read our little story. Additionally, it has helped us understand one another so much better and appreciate the importance of love and family and friends in our lives.

The entire process has undoubtedly been a labor of love.

Contents

Introduction

OUR WEDDING ANNOUNCEMENT appeared in the Styles Section of the Sunday *New York Times* on March 14, 2010.

Ann Vincola and Alan Votta

Ann Patavino Vincola and Alan S. Votta were married Saturday at the Church of God of Prophecy in Charleston, S.C. The Rev. Bernie Levesque, the church's pastor, performed the ceremony.

The bride, 67, will take her husband's name. She owns Tisbury, a shop on Martha's Vineyard in Massachusetts that sells antiques and interior design services. She graduated from SUNY College at Cortland and received a master's degree in administration from Lesley University in Cambridge, Mass. She is a daughter of Helen M. Patavino of Wilbraham, Mass., and the late Carmen A. Patavino.

The bridegroom, also 67, retired as a franchise owner of Chuck Campbell's Wallpaper, Blinds and Decorating Services in Mount Pleasant, S.C. He served 24 years in the Navy, retiring with the rank of chief. He was last stationed at the Fleet Ballistic Missile Submarine Training Center in Charleston. He is a son of the late Anne Votta and the late Alexander Votta, who lived in Yonkers.

The couple met in September 1956, as seventh graders at Charles E. Gorton High School in Yonkers. Mr. Votta followed Ms. Vincola home on the first day of school.

"I waited until she got inside of her house, touched the front steps and promised myself that I would be back," Mr. Votta recalled. "When I first saw her, it was like an instant affection. I spotted her out of this entire entourage of seventh graders. She was just so pretty, she really stood out."

They became friendly over the next few years until they became high school sweethearts during their senior year at Gorton. Their relationship ended the following year when Ms. Vincola went off to college.

Mr. Votta joined the Navy in 1962, married in 1965 and eventually had three children. He became a widower in 2006. He often wondered about his first love.

"The lights went dim, but they never went out," he said about his teenage romance with Ms. Vincola, "All those years, whenever I was feeling down and wanted to cheer myself up, I would think of Ann."

Ms. Vincola married in 1972 and had two children; her marriage ended in divorce in 2000.

In March 2009, the high school sweethearts were reunited when Mr. Votta tracked Ms. Vincola down on Facebook.

"It was wonderful just seeing his name pop up on my phone," she said, "just wonderful."

Both single at the time, they began corresponding by phone and e-mail messages. Two months later, he visited her at her home on Martha's Vineyard and a new romance blossomed.

"It is very powerful to know that after all of these years, someone could still feel a certain way about me," Ms. Vincola said. "We just fit like a glove together."

By VINCENT M. MALLOZZI

Alan is a storyteller. He loves to tell stories—especially our story—over and over and over again. He has gotten quite accustomed to stopping everyone we come in contact with (cashiers at the supermarket, waiters and waitresses, old and new acquaintances, doctors, taxi drivers, *everyone*) about our story. The reaction is always a positive one. It brings a smile to the face and even a tear to the eye—to ours and to the listener's. We have been amazed at how our story has resonated with the masses, as we have met many people who have similar stories and have experienced the wonderful exhilaration of reconnecting with lost love too.

As I contemplated writing it down and sharing the whole story, we were also faced with several personal and family issues that required much thought and considerable struggle. Despite the fact that our reuniting and marrying has resulted in untold pleasure and joy, we were forced to deal with some hard realities of life. We have spent many hours simply talking and listening to one another; making our union even stronger. Our joint soul searching has given us a much better understanding of who we both are and what ultimately matters in our lives and in our future life together. It led me to believe that I really must tell it all—that the *whole* story is compelling enough to be shared with the world. I began jotting down some notes and thought about the general outline of my memoir using the concept of reuniting as my focus.

Although we both are rather private people and we have lived most of our lives quietly, without the need to bring attention to ourselves, our outlook changed when we came together again. I feel certain that some will be surprised that

I have decided to reveal intimate details of our lives, but loving Alan as I do and understanding our strong commitment to one another, I haven't hesitated one minute. I also haven't hesitated to speak about our belief in Divine Intervention. Although we are not seriously religious people, we believe that God has had a hand in it all and we are certain that some of our dearly departed relatives and friends have been instrumental in making our reunion a reality. I also feel that our individual stories, along with our combined story, are more than likely similar to the struggles and the joys that many people have experienced over a lifetime. Thus, the lesson learned, if you will, is that everyone should recognize the importance of individual accomplishments as well as failures, and not live with regret over the decisions we may have made in the past, and believe that there is a silver lining somewhere in the future for all of us.

I determined initially that I would structure the book with the concept of "reuniting" as the foundation; i.e., how *we* reunited, of course, but also that we reunited with family and friends after we reconnected, making it an even more engaging story. I didn't get very far then. But it was a start. It wasn't until almost a year and half after our wedding that I went back to our narrative and then I was committed. I began to work on it in earnest.

Alan and I have been together every single day since just before our engagement party. We have travelled up and down the east coast from Martha's Vineyard to Charleston to Sarasota so many times that we believe the car could navigate on its own. We have fun every day and we laugh a lot. We do everything together and find that we are side by side every minute of the day and night. Did I ever think that I could be that connected to another human being? No! But that is the way it is. We never tire of one another and feel strange if the other is not around. We feel blessed that we have been given this gift of sharing our lives again.

In this era of social media—and since Facebook is what brought us together in the first place—we have become advocates for the benefits of social media outlets, even for oldsters like us! It is what enabled us to reunite and it has allowed us to stay in close contact with the many friends with whom we have since reconnected. We have been astounded at the number of times the announcement of our wedding in *The New York Times,* has been noticed and picked up by other sources. I found the following quote as part of *The Couples Tool Kit:*

> *Facebook has surfaced to introduce the daily possibility of reunions with soul mates from 7th grade. Witness this New York Times piece on the wedding of Ann Patavino Vincola and Alan S. Votta who at 67, after previous marriages and decades apart, were blissfully joined together in holy matrimony. This happy ending was the outcome of Mr. Votta's search for his childhood sweetheart utilizing the services of the 21st Century version of Yenta The Matchmaker, Facebook. It is common knowledge that the baby boomer generation has invaded the once private bastion of college age students with their usual vigor and ferocity.*

It has been an interesting journey. This is the story of how it began, what happened in between, and where we are now.

Martha's Vineyard
October 2011

PART ONE

Our Past

1

Finding Out Who
You Really Are

*I*THINK THAT IT TAKES A LIFETIME to understand what makes you tick and to become fully acquainted with your true self.

This is the story of reconnecting with lost love and the high school sweetheart I let go of over 50 years ago. Lucky me that the story is a good one—one that makes people cry—and one that gives people hope for themselves. In fact, women often say to me once they have heard what happened with us, "Maybe there is hope for ME! Perhaps I should get on Facebook." After all, we reconnected via social networking, i.e. Facebook, and there's no reason that can't happen for others.

It is also a story of reconnecting to our individual pasts and understanding and appreciating what is most important in life. It is a story of reuniting, not only with lost love, but with old friendships and with some of the people who meant a lot to us when we were very young. Someone once said to me that when you reconnect with friends who knew you in high school, it enables you to go back to your true self. I believe that. Furthermore, I had no idea that this simple phrase and this experience of reuniting would ultimately have such a great impact on me.

I most ardently believe that all of our life's experiences—the joys, the highs, the lows, as well as the sorrows and the difficulties—prepare us to evolve into oneself. It has taken all of this and more for me to arrive at a place of pure contentment, love, and peace—no matter what obstacles may still stand in the way. I now know who I am, what is important to me, who and what I love and cherish, and I embrace my values and ideals. I have finally learned to live every day in a way that I hope shows that love and appreciation.

When I divorced in 2000 I made more changes in my life than merely in my marital status. It was a real turning point for me. My ex-husband and I decided in July of 1999 that we would go our separate ways after 27 years of marriage. Honestly, it felt like a huge release for me. I knew that I hadn't been happy, and my life within that marriage was difficult and limiting at best. I was now free to be me again.

After my divorce I spent a year living in a lovely apartment in downtown Boston as I continued with my career as a Work/Life Consultant. I worked with corporate clients developing dependent care benefits and flexible work policies. The job necessitated excessive travel. After a 20-year career as a Work/Life Consultant (and recognized as a pioneer in the field), I was beginning to reassess my position and my relationship to it all. The economy was changing as well and I could see the handwriting on the wall—perhaps it was really time to move on. So—I decided to take a big leap and I left my job, moved to my house on Martha's Vineyard full time, and bought an antique business. It was the third time in my life that I changed course in my career and placed my energies in an entirely different direction. This new venture eliminated all of the travel and the pressures that were put upon me in my previous job. And I was happy to be living on the Vineyard, the place that had always been a refuge for me.

Throughout my entire life I always had a nagging feeling that I didn't quite measure up. And if I couldn't be the *best* at something then it wasn't worth the effort. I always excelled in school, got good grades and was popular. But again, I needed to be the *best*. So I was always striving to be better—thinking that I wasn't doing well enough, and always very concerned about what people thought of me. I presume that most of us feel this way from time to time, but for me it was a driving force. It was true in elementary school, in high school, in college, in my career, and yes, even in my marriage. I worried about others' opinion of me and I continuously looked for acceptance, validation, and approval—particularly from my husband, which didn't come easily.

On the surface it always looked like I had everything; however, I was often uncertain about who I was; where I was going; or whether I had the strength to follow my own convictions. I denied my many accomplishments, and I always felt that I needed to work harder to be better, especially in making my marriage work. It is then that I realized that I needed the validation of my career—where I could be recognized and valued. It became so clear throughout my evolution and maturity that if I had had the support and recognition that I sought as a wife and mother, I wouldn't need the same from my colleagues, clients, and friends. When I left my job I began to reassess many things in my life.

As I found myself on my own again and starting a new life, I also began to get to know myself a lot better. I learned to think for myself. I learned to appreciate who and what I am. I learned to value my hard work. And I learned to like myself better. I no longer worried about what people thought about me. I learned that I was well-liked for myself—me. I learned to trust myself and to trust my own opinions and instincts. I learned to live in the moment and to not sweat the small stuff like I used to. I learned to smell the roses—or the coffee—or whatever there was to smell that would make life exciting for me again. I became much better at enjoying life and understanding that any problem or issue would improve if I gave it enough time. My motto became "It is what it is," something that my mother would consistently say to me on those occasions when things didn't turn out quite the way I had hoped. I became a nicer person to be around. I was more patient. All in all, life became much more pleasant for me and I appreciated all of my many blessings and good fortune instead of waiting for things to get better. I was happy.

I know everyone reaches a point of maturity when things get easier and we are no longer consistently plagued with the question "What do people think of me?" I have always marveled at those people who can speak their mind no matter what the circumstance. My sister-in-law, Donna, could speak her mind to everyone and anyone; people on the street, her parents, friends, her children, her boss, and yes, even her husband. I admired that. She had the ability to say what she felt no matter how outrageous it might be. Whatever was on the tip of her tongue (the kind of thing that most of us would *never* utter) was sure to come out. I would often stand back and watch in awe. I would be amazed at how she could boldly speak out, say what was on her mind, and inevitably stir up controversy. I, on the other hand, would quake in my boots rather than dare utter what was really on my mind. I always thought, "Why can't I do that?" I was too timid. I guess I specialized in a "soft-sell" approach, not necessarily getting to the result I desired. I definitely wished that I could be stronger and be my own advocate in many situations with which I found myself confronted.

Of course, during the years that we were apart Alan lived through his own struggles (most of the time much more difficult than mine) and he continued to think that life could be better if only he tried a little harder. As Alan and I got to know one another once again we both realized that we were very similar in that way. We both kind of let life happen to us rather than taking charge and turning things around to our own advantage. We always seemed to put the needs and desires of others ahead of our personal wants. We strived to make everyone else happy rather than think of our own happiness. This became abundantly clear to us when we had our initial talk with Pastor Bernie Levesque, the man who married us. As we shared with Bernie a little bit about our past and how we both existed prior to our coming together, Bernie said, "Ah ha! You are both 'givers', but you were married to 'takers'. It is when two 'givers' come together that the real magic happens." That made so much sense to us and gave us a lot to contemplate. Maybe that's another reason why we feel so close and so comfortable with one another today. We have also become one another's best advocate and confidence booster. It astonishes me to hear Alan tell me how wonderful I am, and he continues to help me recognize how others appreciate me. I, in turn, am able to do that for him, too. I am constantly in awe of his ability to make people laugh and feel good. It is his gift. And he honestly had lost that for quite some time. Moreover, he had forgotten how to use it to his advantage.

It is an empowering feeling to finally understand one's own psyche and to have arrived at a place of genuine contentment. It is also outrageously invigorating to be able to impart that to others. I am grateful that I have had the opportunity to help Alan understand himself a lot more, and he has done that for me. We feel so lucky to have found one another again, and we plan to continue to provide support and understanding to each other, to our children, and to our family and friends as the years roll on.

So, this is our story. The story of Ann and Alan. There is a lot to tell, but basically it is a love story.

It all started on March 21, 2009 with a Facebook message— a name from the past asking to be my friend.

2

How It All Began—A
Special Year In Our Lives

*A*LAN AND I HAVE known one another since the first
day of seventh grade at Charles E. Gorton High
School, Yonkers, NY. We were the inaugural 7th grade class
to enter the school. In 1956 it was a special place and we felt
lucky and privileged to be there. As we entered 7th grade,
I remember being blown away by the entire atmosphere,
particularly the sophisticated seniors. I loved being there.
I loved my classes, my teachers, my friends—the whole environment. I was thrilled to attend our first pep rally before
the big Thanksgiving Day Game and for me the cheerleaders
were something else altogether. And as a thirteen-year-old
7th grader, I determined then and there that I was going to
be one of them one day.

Gorton *was* a special place. In fact, one of the teachers who attended our 50th high school reunion said to Alan and me that Gorton was a country club or private school kind of atmosphere when we were there. From 1956, when we entered Gorton to 1961 when we graduated, we worked hard at our studies and were taught by exceptional teachers (all graduates of prestigious universities and some even the authors of the very text books we used); they cared about us as individuals. And at the end of the school day we would rush home to turn on the TV and watch Dick Clark's American Bandstand, and practice dancing the Lindy to tunes like Bill Haley's "Rock Around the Clock" and Danny and the Juniors' "At the Hop." How innocent and fun. It was an interesting, simple and carefree era.

Unfortunately, the school environment is no longer the same today. Over the years I realized on numerous occasions, especially in my professional role conducting diversity seminars, that Gorton is the place where I learned how to get along with others and how to appreciate differences. In the late '50s and early '60s Gorton was a microcosm of the real world. It was an insulated safe place where young people learned to respect one another and to appreciate their uniqueness. At the time, North Yonkers, as a suburb of New York City, combined an immigrant population, a growing upper middle class, a black community and an influx of a Jewish population from New York City. We didn't draw attention to our differences; we embraced them and we had fun at the same time. That environment essentially gave us a view of what the real world might look like and, for some of us, we couldn't quite understand the terrible struggles that the civil rights movement would soon bring.

Alan and I are still uncertain just how we got together and started dating. But it had to be sometime in the fall at the very beginning of our senior year. You see, Alan, the great athlete (he played every sport and lettered in all of them), was hurt badly in the first football game of the season that year. In fact, he had to be carried off the field, rushed by ambulance to the hospital, and was hospitalized for almost a month afterward. He suffered a punctured kidney and was unable to play for the rest of the season. My sister, Emma, remembers it all vividly. He had already become her 'big brother' and she was horrified at the thought of him being carried off. It was quite a shocking moment for everyone since he was co-captain of the team (along with his best friends Billy and Bobby) and such a popular guy. Emmie and I distinctly remember that together we visited Alan in the hospital. So whether Alan and I were officially dating by then or not, our close friendship was evident.

What we do remember is that after Alan came back to school following his hospitalization, he walked me home from school one day, carried my books, and from then on we were "the couple." (I never heard the story about his touching the steps of my house on the first day of the seventh grade until he wrote that in an email to me after we reconnected on Facebook.) And so, "we went steady." That's what you did then. We were inseparable. We were together all the time and we spent a lot of time at my house with my family. In those days no one had much money to go out on real dates so we had to be satisfied with the occasional movie or pizza. The only time Alan had a car was when he drove his father to and from a gig: his dad was a drummer. Those were the days when his dad had his own "big band." Wheels or not, our get-togethers were always fun and adventurous. When Alan and I look back at this period of time in our lives we realize how terrific and innocent and happy it was.

Alan floored me with some of the details that came flooding back to him about our time together as we started communicating in emails. He recalled that we went sleigh riding and my mother made us hot chocolate. He reminisced about when he assisted my father in teaching me to drive and laughed at me when I stopped behind a parked car waiting for the traffic to move! He remembered that my mother made Spanish rice that he loved. He remembered that I surprised him with tickets to the Ice Capades at Madison Square Garden to celebrate his birthday just before I set off to Cortland, New York, for my freshman year. And he recalled one evening when we went out to dinner with my mother and father and how he and Dad chuckled when they noticed a patron's very visible toupe rise and fall from the blower on the air conditioner unit every time he bent his head to take a sip of his soup. (Mom and I chastised them for acting so silly.) He recalled that he bought me a ring for Christmas—a black pearl and white pearl; and that I got him a silver ID bracelet, engraved on the back: "with all of my deepest love." He relived the memory of his visit to us when our family vacationed at Sugar Maples in the Catskill Mountains. And he remembered my big extended Italian family—aunts, uncles, cousins, my grandparents, and Zizi (my great aunt) in Mount Vernon, New York.

Alan would walk me home from school every day that he could; that is, if he didn't have basketball or baseball practice or if Miss Azzara, his history teacher, didn't insist that he needed extra study. She would remind him that "Information is *power,* Alan." Sometimes she would even literally open a classroom window and yell out to him as he was leaving school to walk me home. "Votta, get back here! Ann Patavino knows her way home. You should be in here with me, studying."

My father had worked vigorously to renovate our basement to make a fantastic "rumpus room" (or so my mother called it). My Sweet Sixteen party was held there, as well as many other parties including football victory parties; those with a keg of beer in the garage. The drinking age at the time was 18 and we were quite used to having a beer or two—or three—or more, although not all of us were 18 yet. I can't fathom today just how my parents allowed us to hold those parties in our basement. They were especially strict with my sister and me, but somehow they thought it was okay to host the parties. Eventually, a few of those parties got a little out of hand with the police having to be called to quiet things down. But nothing bad ever happened at 199 Morsemere Avenue. At our house it was just good fun. Recently Alan and our friend, Bob, recalled one night when a small group of us got hold of a "Redd Foxx" album and we sat around chuckling at the bawdiness of it. That was about the extent of our bad behavior.

We did share a few serious and sad moments during that year—monumental to a high schooler—but in retrospect, not really that horrendous. They were character builders—so said my mom. I experienced a big disappointment during the spring before we became seniors, which affected our activities the following year. I mentioned before how it had become a supreme goal of mine from the 7th grade when I entered Gorton, to make the cheerleading squad. I wasn't a great athlete in high school and I hadn't yet gotten involved with tennis, which would become an obsession later on. In fact, I hated gym (we had to wear the most horrendous gym suits). But I was a great cheerleader. I had all the moves and, after all, I had been practicing since the 7th grade. I made the squad as a junior—one of only four of us to make it. I had a wonderful time that year and enjoyed every moment as a cheerleader. From all indications I was a shoe-in to be named captain for the following year. During that school year there had also been a personnel change in the Phys Ed department at Gorton. So when tryouts came around in the spring of 1960, I really didn't think much about it. Never before had a junior on the squad not been placed on the squad again. It was the way it was.

Well, I didn't make it.

Only one of the juniors ascended and, naturally, she was named captain. I was devastated. I was heartbroken. How could this be? This was not *right*. Friends were outraged. The football players were outraged. I even remember speaking with Coach Foster, the head football coach, about whether he could do anything. The new gym teachers made their decision and that was it. My sister reminded me (after Alan and I reconnected) that she even wrote a story about what happened for a paper in her 8th grade English class. I was amazed to realize that in her young mind she was convinced that the two Italian-Americans on the cheering squad were discriminated against and were kept off the squad by the two new gym teachers. I, of course, had never given *that* a thought. I just knew that I was robbed of my official right and it took quite a while to get over it (if I ever really did). It pleased me, though, to think that my sister had devised her own analysis of the situation and, who knows, maybe she was right.

So I entered my senior year not as a cheerleader. And after that first football game, Alan was not a football player. Maybe that is another reason why we got together; neither of us had practice to go to after school in the fall of that year.

The other two heartbreakers occurred at the very end of our senior year. One was at our Senior Prom.

The prom was a much-anticipated event and Alan and I had been nominated for King and Queen. Again, the customary way of things was that the most popular couple would be crowned. My friend, Kathy, and her boyfriend, Buzzy, had been king and queen the previous year. Kathy was at my house when a group gathered there for pictures before our prom and she said to me, "I know you will be queen!"

The prom was a wonderful event. I had been to two other senior proms before my own, but this one was truly a special occasion. The evening was a dream. It was held at the Pleasantville Country Club, a lovely location. Alan and I were in love and we danced and danced to romantic songs like The Platters' "Harbor Lights" and "Moments to Remember" by The Four Freshmen. When the class officers announced the king and queen and placed the crown on the heads of Alan as king and someone else and *not me* as queen, I stood there stunned, flabbergasted and hurt beyond belief. Never before had *that* happened—that people voted separately and not for a couple. Alan didn't know what to do and he kept a secret for a very long time—a secret he finally revealed to me in our emails 50 years later! After the crowning and the shock finally wore off for both of us, we continued on with the evening and enjoyed the rest of our Senior Prom weekend, but I was deflated, to say the least. Alan was to learn something about the whole situation later that year on our graduation night.

The biggest disappointment for us came on graduation night. In New York State one needed to pass the regents exam in all subjects in order to receive a regents diploma and graduate. Alan struggled at times with his studies because, as he was later to find out, he was dyslexic. It wasn't until he reached the Navy and excelled in engineering and building nuclear submarines that he understood his true intellect. When Alan took the regents exam it seems that he misread the instructions (which was crazy because he was so prepared for that exam) and instead of choosing three out of five essay questions to write on, he started with number one and attempted to answer them all, but, of course, he didn't complete the exam in the time allotted. Miss Azzara was crushed. She had worked so hard with him and he would have passed the exam easily if he had followed the directions. Fact is that Alan was better prepared for that regents exam than I was. He even tutored me on some of the history facts that were sort of jumbled in my mind. I had Miss Reilly for History. I was in what today would be an AP class and her class was *hard;* and she scared the shit out of me. We both were well-prepared for that exam and except for the glitch of his not following directions, Alan probably would have done better on it than me, the Honor Society student.

The interesting thing about it all is that our very close friend, Gary, didn't pass the regents exam either. So both Alan and Gary, the vice president and the treasurer of our senior class, did not graduate with the rest of us. They couldn't attend the practice sessions for the graduation ceremony and they weren't going to march with their classmates to get their diploma. We got through the ceremony and pictures were taken. Alan's older sister, Anne, found pictures that their father had taken of that night at Gorton. Alan's younger sister, Adrienne, was also in our class and she and I stood on either side of Alan—Teenie and I in our cap and gown and Alan in a suit—a picture that reveals his deep disappointment and sadness that night. He could barely smile. His face held a stern resolute look, which reflected how badly he felt.

Both Alan and Gary stood at the rear of the auditorium and watched as their classmates moved on. Of course, they both easily reversed things that summer and received their diploma, although it was a belated achievement. What we both remember most vividly of that night was attempting to go out and party with our friends, but not feeling much joy in our hearts to do that. I felt all of Alan's pain so acutely. We sat in the car and I was able to hold him in my arms as he cried and cried and let his pain and disappointment wash over him. There was to be another time that he would weep in my arms in that way. (That would happen 50 years later, after our first face-to-face meeting in 2009 when we sat on the sofa in my living room on Martha's Vineyard and Alan told me all about his daughter, Cheryl.)

The information that Alan revealed to me on that graduation night was that I had really been named queen of the senior prom! It seemed that Miss Rowland, the class advisor, who was present at the crowning, felt so badly for Alan on graduation night that in order to make him feel better she told him what actually happened on our prom night. She said that the voting had been in my favor, but for some reason a few female classmates rigged the voting so that I wouldn't get it. How dumbfounded was I to hear that! I think that was another instance when general opinion was that I had it all and why should I also be crowned queen of the senior prom, too. Jealousy? Maybe. But I certainly never thought of myself as having it all. Alan relayed all of this to me in our first emails to one another. Alan didn't know how to react himself. Should he tell me? Should he make an issue of it? He kind of feels guilty about it now and has said that he should have abdicated. But what was an 18-year-old guy supposed to do upon hearing such news? I don't know whether I would have preferred to know about it over these years or to have just dealt with it as I have—as another "character builder." Once he finally told me about it, he felt relieved—no longer holding a secret he kept for fifty years.

Another unique and special aspect of that year we spent together was the beautiful relationship that Alan and my father developed. My father was a very particular and precise man. He took pride in his home and especially his yard. He worked all day every Saturday to mow, weed, enhance, repair and beautify 199 Morsemere Avenue. My sister and I remember it all so well. We had our own household chores to complete on Saturday mornings and we weren't allowed to leave the house or do anything else until the chores were finished and inspected by Dad.

It seems that my father recognized in Alan the same kind of attention to detail and precision of work. I can attest to that today. I am amazed at Alan's neatness, preciseness, and ability to fix anything and everything, just like my dad. Thus, the only person that my father ever trusted enough to help him with his work around the house was Alan. Dad allowed Alan to mow the lawn for him, but only after he gave Alan a half hour instruction as to where the undulations were in the lawn and how the mower had to carefully move over them. Dad also asked Alan to help him build and paint an arbor over the slate patio in the backyard, which became one of the focal points of our very lovely yard and the spot where we enjoyed many family gatherings and celebrations.

In addition, Dad trusted Alan to drive his car—really quite a big deal. My father had been in the automotive business all his life and knew everything there was to know about cars. And just like his yard, he took great pride in his automobiles. Alan retells the story of when I returned home from Cortland that very first Thanksgiving vacation in November of 1961. Alan was already back at home in Yonkers from Hofstra University, and was waiting for my arrival along with my parents. My father threw Alan the keys to his '57 Chevy and told him to "go get her." No one else drove my father's car.

Alan elaborated on that story and described a rather touching scene that he remembered vividly when he began his reminiscing on everything about that year. When Alan picked me up at LaGuardia Airport he was allowed on the tarmac as the little prop plane landed. While he waited for the plane to land, he had befriended the security guard at the gate explaining to the guard that he was there to pick up his girlfriend. As the plane was taxiing, Alan saw the guard at another doorway waving to Alan to get his attention. He secretly snuck Alan through the gate and onto the tarmac. I was the third person off the plane. We ran across the tarmac into each other's arms. While we were embracing, kissing, and spinning around as Alan lifted me in his arms, Alan noticed the security guard watching—with tears in his eyes, and leading the applause as several other passersby enjoyed the scene too.

As a family, my parents and sister and I vacationed at a place in the Catskill Mountains called Sugar Maples. We would take a week (a week was all we could afford) in July during my father's vacation. Sugar Maples became a very special place for all of us. The first few years we went there we stayed in the main house—in one shared room with a hall bath. We started going there when I was a young teenager—probably fourteen. It is where I learned to play and love the game of tennis. My father was an excellent tennis player and he had wanted his daughters to get into the game. I showed an interest and discovered that I could hit the ball pretty well. It was at Sugar Maples that I got hooked. I would watch my father play with the men and then, as I was invited to play in father/daughter matches, I learned to love it too.

But that's not all there was to Sugar Maples. We made friends. We went on hayrides. We ate in the dining room for three meals a day: we went to the casino at night to dance; and we swam in the pool every day. It was a fairyland for us. Emmie and I absolutely loved all of it, as did my parents. Lifelong family friends were made there too. The last time we went to Sugar Maples as a family was my senior year and Alan came up for an overnight visit before we left for home. So Alan got to experience the magic of Sugar Maples with us as well. He remembers staying overnight in housing where the "help" stayed—just like in the movie "Dirty Dancing." Everything about Sugar Maples was like "Dirty Dancing!" Alan felt very fortunate to be allowed to share that wonderful place with my family.

If I am painting a picture of a very special time in our lives, that is my intention. Alan became part of the family. He teased his "little sister" unmercifully—calling her Brillo Head—but she loved it. And Alan had a special bond with my mother too. He tells me now that he always thought she was so beautiful, that she always looked nice. He remembers her hair and her smile. One incident sticks out in his mind. During the Christmas holiday the year that we were dating, Alan was encouraged to stop and have a bit of "Christmas Cheer" at several neighbors' or friends' homes as he walked to my house. By the time he finally reached my house Alan was full of *cheer*. My mother answered the door and recognized immediately that Alan was "two sheets to the wind," as she would say. She laughed and ushered him into the house and filled him with several cups of coffee before he was allowed to join the others gathered there.

Alan also remembers how sensitive Mom was when he would visit my parents after we broke up. After he joined the Navy he visited them in Hartsdale whenever he was home and able to get there. They always welcomed him warmly and my mother informed him of whatever was going on in my life at the time. In retrospect, I think that Dad, as a veteran who served in World War II, was pleased that Alan had joined the military. Dad respected Alan for that, adding to what drew them close to one another.

Alan also shared with me that from time to time he would find himself parked across the street from the Morsemere Avenue house and just sit and think about the past and what it had meant to him. It made him feel better and he continued to do that for years. His memories of that one year in our lives and the subsequent times he visited with my parents were beginning to come alive for him again. One of the stories that Alan tells nowadays (to everyone who will listen to him about how we got together again) also reveals the closeness that my parents felt with Alan. My 94 year old mother, when told that I had been in touch with Alan once again, said, "You mean the man I *thought* was going to be your *husband*?"

So, you see, he was fully accepted into our very close-knit family and now that we are together again, everyone is extremely happy to have him back. My mother has the biggest smile on her face whenever he appears when we visit her at her assisted living complex and she delights in having him near. The only regret that I have is that my father is no longer with us to enjoy it all. But somehow I am sure that he is aware that we are together again and is smiling down on us every day.

In fact, I'm sure he had a part in making it all happen. Alan often jokingly looks up to the heavens and calls, "Carmen!" when I have done something outrageous or when I have come out with what he calls another Annie-ism, and he comically seeks my father's help in dealing with me.

Our individual stories, and what happened to each of us from 1962 to 2009 sets the stage for our beautiful reunion.

3

Alan's Story

ALAN'S STORY is a tough one. It is difficult for me to
think about everything that he endured during his life
from December 1961 until we reunited. And, although I'm not
to blame, I can't help feeling responsible to some extent. He
went through some very rough periods. Nevertheless, the one
thing I am eternally grateful for is that he was able to remain
whole and his spirit didn't die. Today, the fun-loving, silly,
wonderful person he was in high school has been reawakened
for the world to behold. After all, he *was* named "Most Popular"
at Gorton and *everyone* just loves him. And I am continually
reintroduced to "Mr. Personality" every day when we meet
someone when we are shopping at Costco, for instance, who
may have worked with Alan at Home Depot, or was part of
his life in some other way. He stops; tells our story to everyone—starting off with—"50 years ago she broke off with me…"

I am always startled at how Alan can engage anyone in a conversation and get a laugh. For instance, in a check-out line in the supermarket he might make an offhand remark that will certainly get a reaction. He has an innate sense of just how far he can go. Some might take his comments as a direct insult or as a racial slur, but he always gets a laugh. Early on in our new relationship I sometimes found myself cringing at his outspokenness, but I would be amazed at the humorous banter that usually resulted, followed by uproarious laughter. What he had to say worked. Alan's assessment is, "I just know how far I can go and if I feel I will get a negative response, I don't go there." Given his personality, it seems we are forever having a great time with everyone whom we come in contact. His public absolutely *loves* him, as do all of our old and new friends, as we continue on this road of reconnecting.

To begin. When I broke off with Alan during that Christmas vacation of my freshmen year, while we were at home in Yonkers, Alan was completely shattered. I can still remember his face when I told him that I wished to date other people. I knew that I was hurting him, but I did not know to what extent. As he tells it, he had no other thought in his head than that we would marry after we finished college and live happily ever after. I must also add here that in no way at that time had we been intimate at all; we just kissed and hugged a lot. It was 1960, after all, and I was a goody-two-shoes. Alan, of course, being a guy, had had his share of experiences; but in 1960/61 he respected me so much that he felt very comfortable waiting until we were married. I was going to be his *wife*.

Instead, I pulled the rug from under him. We still saw one another during the rest of that vacation and then I returned to Cortland and he to Hofstra. What I learned all these years later was that Alan could not cope once he returned to Hofstra, and he left school soon after that (it was really just a matter of weeks). He packed up and went back to Yonkers to his parents' house. He realized that was a mistake, and found himself in a Navy recruiter's office after checking out the Marine Corps and knowing that wasn't for him either. He was given several tests which he passed with flying colors. He learned about the new nuclear submarine Navy, and the incredible future he might have as part of it. This piqued his interest and he soon enlisted. He called this his French Foreign Legion and his way of trying to forget me and move on. During this time when he went through basic training and his initial school-ing in submarine school, he continued to visit my parents in Yonkers, and then visited them in Hartsdale where they moved while I was still in college. I think my parents were very disappointed that I had moved on without Alan as my boyfriend, and during those years the three of them continued to develop a very special bond. I was completely unaware that he had continued to see them and I just went on happily with my very social days at Cortland.

Alan continued in submarine school and excelled at every turn. He had originally expected that he would remain in the Navy for three years, and then go back to college and finish his education. Instead he found himself with seven years under his belt in the Navy. He was entrenched in building subma-rines and eventually became a Naval Instructor. During that time he was stationed in several places, but found himself in Charleston, South Carolina, at the outset of his Navy career and he would continue to return there until his eventual retirement from the Navy in 1983 after almost twenty-four years of service.

When he was in Newport News, Virginia, and beginning to build submarines, he met his first wife. As he still tells it today, she was nice, attractive, and from a good family. And he got involved. It was certainly time for him to have a relationship and think about a romantic attachment. They started dating and they were soon talking about marriage. What wasn't revealed at the outset of their relationship was that she had already given birth to three children that she had conveniently given up to others to care for (one to her first husband's parents, one to her own parents, and the last one to a friend). When Alan learned of this he was dumbfounded to say the least. Initially, she had only revealed to Alan that Joey was her son, and the fact that she had given birth to two other children was revealed later on. But being the kind of person that Alan is, he decided that he would still try to make it work. He told her that she should get Joey back and that they would make a family together. That happened and Joey was returned to their care. Alan fell in love immediately with the adorable, tow-headed, little one-year-old.

His wife became pregnant once again (this time with Alan's child). She blamed Alan for forcing her to marry him, although she had conveniently neglected to take the birth control pills he was instrumental in getting for her after he had gotten her to see a doctor for the first time in years. And so they married. After, that is, Alan paid for her divorce from Joey's father. Of course, that was another thing that she didn't reveal when they first started seeing one another—that she was still married. More was to surface and Alan found himself deep into an untenable situation. A friend of ours recently had this to say when the story was relayed to him: "Perhaps after having been rejected from the relationship that he believed was to be forever, he felt that he had to settle, that he wasn't going to find anything better." I believe that there is something to that because Alan continued to place himself into very difficult situations from which he was never able to extricate himself.

After they married they moved to Uncasville, Connecticut, where Alan continued his studies at Fleet Ballistic Missile Submarine School on the Groton Navy Base and was stationed on the George C. Marshall Submarine SSBN654. Janice gave birth to Alan's son, Stephen, in 1967. So their family consisted then of Alan, his wife, Joey, and Steve. Alan was a willing, loving father and he was doing all in his power to keep his family intact. However, his wife had other ideas. She continued to play around and was continually unfaithful to Alan. They were relocated to Mare Island, California, and she became pregnant again. Cheryl was born when they returned to Charleston after his assignment in California. At this point his wife could care less about a new baby and she didn't want to have much to do with the two boys either. Unfortunately, Cheryl entered this world without any crucial bonding with her mother.

Alan's wife continued to display rather wandering tendencies, had several affairs, and finally informed Alan that she did not want to be a wife or a mother any longer. This is what

Alan was waiting for. He had known for a very long time, although he had tried valiantly to make things work, that they never would. He generously helped to move her out of their house and set her up in her own apartment, while Alan and Joey and Steve and Cheryl remained in their home. A year later she was served with divorce papers and the marriage was over. Alan continued on with his life—caring for their three children alone.

He tried his damndest to keep things going while still in the Navy, but it became exceedingly difficult, especially with assignments at sea. Believing that he could make it all work if he didn't have to leave the kids, he decided to leave the Navy. He took a job as a civilian engineer at Vitro Laboratories in Silver Springs, Maryland. Alan and the children remember this time as one of the best. He loved his kids and he was a super father—as difficult as it was on a daily basis. He worked hard and with the aid of sitters and day care, their family survived. The boys were fine. They were a bit older by then. But it was more difficult for Cheryl. She would sometimes wander off and not stay with sitters. Alan worried about her a great deal because he was fully aware that she never got the kind of mothering every newborn baby needs and that she required more feminine nurturing. However, the Navy came calling again. The Navy wanted Alan back. And they offered him a situation where he would not have to go to sea. He moved his family back to Charleston, South Carolina, and Alan was again a Navy man.

And that is when the real horror story began—the one that lasted for 30 years with "The Evil One," as his second wife was not-so-affectionately called by Steve and Catherine, Alan's son and daughter-in-law. Living in Charleston while caring for three young children and serving in the Navy, Alan began attending Parents Without Partners meetings. He was, understandably, a rather popular addition to the group and found himself very much in demand for dates as well as for serving on committees. It was at this point that he met his second wife. She had one son by a previous marriage and she ran a small beauty shop. Although she was ten years older than Alan, they began dating. I believe that they both saw in each other a solution to their problems and a way to make their individual living situations somewhat better. Was there love? From what I now know, I do not think so at all. I think it was just a convenience for each of them and, very honestly, a necessity for Demitria because she was having such a difficult time financially. They decided to marry. Prior to Alan entering her life, she needed to rent out a room in her home to make ends meet. So after they married, Alan was able to take over all of the household expenses, including paying the mortgage. Alan thought that he now had someone to share in the care of his children. However, as he was soon to find out, his new wife was really not the mothering or nurturing kind, and she took advantage of Alan—using his skill, his love, and his money. From the beginning Alan took over most of the household chores and care of the four children. She was much happier being at her beauty shop where she remained most nights until about 9 PM. The kids were *tolerated* in the house by her and they spent most of their time in their respective bedrooms when she was around. They learned early on to stay out of her way in order to not cause a scene or be on the receiving end of her demeaning wrath. She never celebrated birthdays, and holidays were tension-filled at best.

Alan blindly fell into it. In fact, his new wife had another story in her past that absolutely flabbergasted me when Alan relayed it to me. As a mother myself, I will never be able to understand why or how she could do what she did.

Demi had been married twice before she married Alan. She divorced both men. Both marriages were miserable failures and both of her ex-husbands despised her. Alan really should have known better than to get involved in the first place. But once again, he let life happen to him rather than to orchestrate it for himself. Her second husband was Peter's father. She was married to her first husband for about seven years. Originally from New York, she started as a beautician there. Being of Greek heritage she became part of the Greek community wherever she lived. She did not get pregnant with her first husband, but she wanted a child. She and her husband were already having difficulties in their marriage and, unbeknownst to him, she travelled to Greece and came home with a baby that she adopted there. Her husband was furious that she had adopted a child without his knowledge, but he tried to make the new family work. The difficulties between them continued to mount and soon they found themselves divorcing. However, there was the question of the child and which of them would get custody of her. Having had such a difficult time with his wife when she adopted the baby in Greece, he desired to get the upper hand in a situation that was impossible for him from the beginning. By this time the little girl was four years old.

Demitria wanted her for herself and took the child and fled to Mexico where she lived for almost a year and a half until their whereabouts was discovered. That is when she moved to Charleston, South Carolina. Her husband set up a false residency in Georgia to hire some backwoods lawyers to make a plea on his behalf. He was awarded custody of the child and Demi lost her to her utter dismay. It was then that she met her second husband, Peter's father. Her life with him was no better than with her first husband. They were married for only about four years. But she finally got pregnant and then had a child to love, to pamper, to spoil, and to give everything to.

Demi was not an easy person to live with. She found fault in everyone and in every situation. If someone tried to assist her with anything, she would accuse them of thinking that she was stupid; showing her paranoia in all encounters. Her needs and desires took precedence over anything else. For example, on Saturday mornings when Alan would typically mow the lawn and do other chores around the house, she would follow him outside and complain that he was abandoning her. And when he came back inside to placate her, she would get upset because the grass never got cut. She displayed the classic argumentative personality—if you said the sky is blue, she would say it is black. She could be termed a control freak!

I must say once again, now knowing the full story, that I don't think there was a time (even at the beginning of their marriage) when there was love, true compatibility, and sharing. Alan always seemed to think that things would get better. If he tried harder, they would get better. But he was with a woman who couldn't get along with *anyone*—even her own family. Her two brothers felt that she was incorrigible and her New York actor brother twice tried to convince Alan to leave her. Both brothers are since deceased.

Alan never seemed to find a way to get out of a bad marriage and a difficult situation. To this day he cannot understand why he was unable to do that. He felt that it was up to him to try to make the situation better and that he should work harder at it.

The real tragedy of Alan's marriage to Demi, however, involves Alan's daughter, Cheryl. Before they had married, Alan realized that he was not providing Cheryl the parenting she required and he had asked his parents in Yonkers if they would take her for a while. Cheryl lived with Anne and Alexander Votta for a year until they felt that they were unable to keep on caring for her. It seems she continued wandering off at times which became too difficult for Alan's parents to handle. And each time she was under Alan's care, Cheryl's behavior continued to be problematic and he worried about her constantly. Cheryl then spent some time with her other grandparents, in Arkansas, at the time when Alan married Demi. Missing her own daughter, Demi suggested that they bring Cheryl back to live with them. Alan thought that this might finally be the loving family situation that Cheryl needed and she would finally be with her brothers again and with him, her father. Alan tells me now that as soon as Cheryl walked into the house he saw the look on his wife's face and knew that it was a horrible mistake. She was in no way going to bring this "other" daughter into her domain. And that is when the horrible stuff started. Alan's wife made life miserable for Joey, for Steve, but especially for Cheryl.

They all retell a story about "when the bikes were stolen at Christmas." All four children received bikes for Christmas. But within four or five days, the bikes were stolen from the open storage area at the back of their yard where they had been left. Apparently the culprits had crossed over from the movie theater at the mall across the road and entered the neighborhood and took them. Only Peter got a replacement bike. And that's the way it was all the time. Peter got all the attention. Peter got everything—including love and affection—even from Alan. As Catherine (Alan's daughter-in-law who was the one who put him onto Facebook) revealed to me in an early email when she tried to give me some insight into the family situation, "When Alan married Demi, Peter got a loving father, but Steve and Joey got less than zero!"

They lived with the Evil Stepmother. But it was most difficult for Cheryl. They all admit now that there was abuse, both verbal and physical. For example, if Cheryl tried to climb up onto Alan's lap, Demi would get upset and start screaming at both Cheryl and Alan and label Cheryl's behavior as precocious. It was clear that Demi was jealous of Cheryl and that manifested itself in not allowing Alan to be a loving father to his daughter. Demi would take Cheryl's dolls away to punish her. It was impossible for Demi to show any kind of love and affection toward Cheryl and any time Cheryl would seek that from Alan, Cheryl would be chastised and punished and confined to her room. Demi was the evil stepmother personified.

Alan didn't know what to do. He knew that his daughter could not remain in this environment and he understood that he should get himself out of this unbearable mess of a marriage. But how? He had tried once before to care for three children on his own and it was nearly impossible. He felt that he and the boys could cope one way or the other. But Cheryl needed something different, at least until she was old enough to make some decisions for herself. He desperately wanted to make the right decision for the daughter he loved so. Someone had told him about the foster care route and he mentioned it to his wife. She thought that was a suitable alternative and went about setting up an appointment. Alan then found himself sitting at a foster care office with her and signing papers that would take Cheryl away from him—as he believed—for a period of time, which would give her a better chance in life. At the time the foster care arrangement was different than what I believe it to be today. A sobbing Alan signed the papers with his stoic wife urging him on as the only thing he could do. The next day he realized he had made a horrible mistake and he tried to undo it. But he learned that there was nothing he could do. She was gone. And from that day forward she has been out of his life. The heartache continues.

And the marriage continued. Alan opened a pawn shop. They were in the antique business together. Alan bought a house on the Edisto River and worked hard to fix it up as their River House. The boys grew. Alan and his wife opened a franchise business, Chuck Campbell Wallpaper and Blinds, in Mount Pleasant, South Carolina. Alan got his broker's license. He bought and sold properties and successfully flipped real estate, making it a profitable business for them. And Demi continued to be her difficult self. It seemed that they lost every friend they ever had because of her miserable personality. In fact, one friend of Demi's once called Alan on the phone and tried to convince him to be stronger in his attitude toward Demi and try to control her better by force if necessary; that she needed some reining in and that physically overpowering her should be considered! Of course, that was never Alan's style and he would be incapable of doing anything like that.

There was even tension in her beauty shop. She would control the schedule and overbook and then intimidate and scare customers into submission. On one occasion when Alan stopped in to the shop, he witnessed a customer in tears because she was afraid of Demi's wrath. To this day, people unwittingly reveal to me how they disliked her and how difficult it was to get along with her. She apparently had a superior attitude about herself and thought that everyone she came in contact with was beneath her. Most people were uncomfortable in her presence. She had a strange way of alienating everyone she encountered with her cold and calculating personality.

In fact, at this time because of the difficulties they were already having in their marriage, Alan believed they should consult a marriage counselor and Demi agreed to seek professional help. The marriage counselor, a clinical psychologist, essentially diagnosed Demi as a borderline paranoid schizophrenic. After several sessions (one-on-one and together as a couple) the doctor, speaking individually to Alan said, "Your wife refuses to be treated and has refused further counseling or medication. I can't really do much more for her and, unprofessionally speaking, she's fucking crazy." Totally dumbfounded, Alan realized he was in far deeper than he ever expected, and he didn't quite know what to do.

To compound issues, following the sessions with the psychologist, Alan had caught his wife in a compromising situation with a female customer of hers in the beauty parlor she operated. Alan had gone to pick her up after she worked late one night and he had the three boys with him in the car. They had recently installed window film on the windows. Demi didn't quite understand how this new substance on the windows worked: she thought she was hiding from the world inside the shop at night; however, the reverse was true. During the day one could see out, but no one could see in. At night when the light was brighter inside, one could see very clearly what was going on in there. Alan was very shocked to see what he saw and told the boys to get back in the car. He went into the shop and confronted her. She was outraged that she was caught. Needless to say, there was not much intimacy in their marriage either before or after this incident; nor, for that matter, during most of the 30 years that they were together.

Alan packed up lock, stock and barrel and moved out of their house. Joey, Steve, and Alan left and when Demi realized it, she made an attempt to patch things up, which consisted mainly of dropping Peter off to be with the boys. Essentially she was dumping Peter off to free up her own time. Peter did not want to go back to his mother and begged to stay with Alan and the boys. This got to be such a bad scene that Alan weakened and thought that he could, perhaps, make an impossible situation bearable. So, for Peter's sake, Alan stayed in the marriage. However, he soon acknowledged that he had been such a fool and he was continuing to be a victim all over again.

Alan was trapped. For the next ten years Alan stood by a woman who was a monster. But, once again, his basic instinct was to do what he believed to be the right thing even if it destroyed him.

Alan felt that as soon as all of the boys were of age and out of the house, he would be able to leave and get out too. He had lost Cheryl, but he felt a strong responsibility to make a good loving home for the boys. When Alan and Demi sold their business they were able to build a beautiful house on the marsh in West Ashley. All the while Alan kept on with the same thinking: "If I work hard, things will improve." But they never did. They got worse. They lived separately in that big house. Alan went to work at Home Depot, so that he could get out of the house and away from her. There he could be Alan, the fun-loving, warm, and generous soul that people love. And love him, they did. In fact, several of the young people that he worked with at Home Depot came to our wedding. He was their father figure. He took them all under his wings. That was his life.

It was then that he felt it was time. Time to leave. However, life had other plans. Demitria began showing signs that something was wrong physically. She suffered from Thalosimia, a blood disease that affects people of Greek descent. She continued to weaken. Alan did everything at home—all of the cooking, all of the cleaning, all of the shopping. Alan cared for her. And the task of driving her to and from medical appointments also fell upon him, as well as getting her to her bead shop, the last business venture she operated. Alan was there at the ready to do what needed to be done.

During this time, Peter married Cynthia and they had a child, Britton. Alan had continued to be the loving father to Peter all these years and now became the loving "Papou" to Britton from the day he was born. In fact, Alan became Britton's chief caregiver during his early years, while Cynthia and Peter worked. When Britton was an infant, Cynthia or Peter dropped Britton off at Alan's house and Alan would prepare Britton for a trip to Demi's shop. At the shop Alan again checked Britton's needs, for a diaper change or a bottle, before himself departing to begin his work day. Britton was cared for at the shop by a young girl, the daughter of another shop owner nearby. The young girl's mother would bring her to work with her and the girl would be Demi's strength (since her illness she couldn't cope with much) until Peter or Cynthia came by in the afternoon to take Britton home with them. Of course, on Alan's days off Britton automatically stayed with Alan at home.

Alan and Britton formed an exceptional bond. After Cynthia and Peter's very contentious divorce, Cynthia affirms that it was she and Alan who raised that child. Britton loves his Papou. He continues to jump into his arms every time he sees him. When I entered the picture Britton still figured greatly in Alan's life and I loved seeing them together. What a pair! And now that is the other big tragedy in Alan's life: a break with his stepson. Peter has made it virtually impossible for Britton to see his Papou on a regular basis. The break was essentially caused by the sad state of affairs of Alan and Demitria's marriage.

During the time she was ill, Alan was caught once again. His wife continued to fail and she needed him. There was no way that he could take off then. Alan was unaware that she was also seeing an oncologist, the only medical appointment she went to without Alan. It seems that the Thalosimia developed into full-blown leukemia. She was hospitalized several times and the back and forth was very trying for both of them. In the midst of all of this, Alan required two hip replacements and a knee replacement and he had to care for himself each time he was discharged from the hospital after his surgery. I had two hip replacements myself and I can't imagine coming home from the hospital without help. He basically healed himself and did his own physical therapy.

Unexpectedly, Demi passed away after being admitted to the hospital the last time. That was in February 2007. Alan stayed by her side faithfully and nursed her and took care of her every need until the day she died. And he did it without malice.

After she passed Alan got on with his life as best he could. It was really the same as it had been before she died. He had all the responsibilities of his home; he cared for Britton on almost a daily basis; and he worked part-time at Home Depot. He was, though, released from the bondage that he had endured. But what was his life? He felt content. And he felt that he would just go on and make the most of it all. He recalls that a neighbor woman came into the house one day after learning that Alan had been recently widowed. After walking through the house and eyeing the beautiful view of the marsh out back, she informed him that "she could get used to that" and he should give her a call and they would go out to dinner. He ushered her to the door and shut it tightly behind her. There was no way that he was going to get involved again and he had no interest whatsoever in having any woman enter his life. He felt that he would be happy doting on his grandchildren and having a meal once in awhile at Steve and Catherine's—after all, Steve was a graduate of the Culinary Institute and both Catherine and Steve are exceptional cooks.

But one dark issue still loomed. Shortly after Alan's wife passed, Peter had come rushing into the house frantically looking for *The Will*. Alan didn't even know that a will existed. This is where the sticky story begins and it is the reason that Alan has severed ties with his stepson, Peter. A court case followed. The gist of the story is that Demitria had prepared a will that Alan didn't know a thing about, but Peter knew *exactly* what was contained in it.

She had met with a lawyer in secret following a row with Alan's son, Steve, in 2000. Shortly before that, Steve had asked for a copy of his parents' tax return so that he could continue with a Pell Grant at Clemson where he had been a student for three years. His stepmother refused to give that to him, which resulted in Steve needing to drop out of college. It was another example of Alan's inability to stand up to his wife and come to his son's aid. At one point after that Steve wrote to his father explaining how he felt about many things.

Dad, There really is no hatchet to bury. I thought I made it clear when I had my 'discussion' with Dee that you were welcome in my life. The problem is that

I want absolutely nothing to do with that woman. I don't ever want to speak with her again and that is never going to change...Dee has manipulated so many people's lives to her own selfish wishes. When she didn't get her way she took drastic measures, i.e. Nicolette to Mexico; 'disposing' of Cheryl, extorting your rights to the river house...etc. She is a controlling, self-absorbed person and I despise her. I resent you for being so weak as to let a person like that control you for all these years.

Following that incident—and what ultimately became the crux of the matter—Demitria wanted to ensure that *nothing* of their combined estate would *ever* be left to Steve. Thus, she had a will prepared that left everything to her son Peter. Because, as a married couple, they had been in business together, the customary rule of thumb at the time was to put everything (property, etc.) in the wife's name to protect assets if anything had happened to the business. The will outlined all of their assets (marital home, river house, Peter's home and property, commercial properties, cars, cash, jewelry, etc.). Thus, all of their assets were in his wife's name.

Alan was left with only half of the value of his home, and everything else that he had worked so hard for during his life was given to Peter.

Of course, it is important to note here that over the years, Alan had paid for everything himself (all mortgages and household expenses). Alan was shocked when he understood what was happening. However, at this same time his father was ill in New York and he needed to make several trips up north to see him. Alexander Votta passed away in June of 2007, just a few months after Demi died.

The will was in probate and Peter had asked his stepdad whether he was going to contest the will. Alan, being the kind of guy he is, and, frankly, unable to focus on the reality of it all at the time, felt that he and Peter would work everything out together, and that they would find an equitable solution to the unjust contents of his mother's will. Thus, Alan did nothing and did not contest it. Alan felt that he and Peter had a loving relationship and all would be worked out; how could Peter not understand that a gross injustice had been done to him? All his life's work and assets were given to Peter, his stepson. So, stupidly, Alan let things lie, although he continually said to Peter, "We need to talk." However, Peter never found the time to do that and nothing changed. That is when Alan began putting it all down on paper and he wrote the first letter to Peter imploring him to pay attention to him and look at the situation.

At that time, Alan also decided to write a letter to Cheryl in an attempt to make amends and see if there was any way that reconciliation could occur. Cheryl had been adopted when she was about ten years old by a loving couple and lived in South Carolina, before moving to Miami. She has lived a happy and productive life, which is what Alan had hoped for her. She is a registered nurse, is married to a wonderful guy and has a son, Nicholas. In 2005 Steve, again with Catherine's intervention and help, found Cheryl and they have reunited and now maintain a loving relationship. All Alan hoped for was to be able to see Cheryl once again and for her to know that he loves her and has loved her every day of her life and only wanted the best for her.

Peter was totally unreceptive to Alan's pleas and would have none of it. He even sent some scathing responses to Alan that hurt Alan deeply. And Cheryl has yet to respond, communicating through Steve and Catherine that she is not quite ready. We live in hope. Small steps in communication have begun such as "liking" each other on Facebook, allowing us to at least keep up with the happenings in one another's lives. We hope that little by little she will agree to a meeting.

Several more letters followed between Peter and Alan with the same disrespectful responses until Alan determined that there was nothing else he could do but sever ties with Peter and Amy (Peter's second wife). Following that, the inevitable occurred and a court case ensued. Knowing that the outcome might ultimately be a futile attempt to set things right, Alan thought that it just might wake Peter up to the grave injustice. Alan finally hired a lawyer to represent him. It became a nightmare and a terrible end to a relationship with a stepson whom Alan raised from five years of age. The other consequence is that Alan no longer saw Britton as much as he would like and doesn't have the important influence on his life that he once enjoyed. Thankfully, the relationship with Cynthia, Britton's mother, is a positive one, and she has enabled us to see Britton whenever possible and stay in close touch.

And because I entered Alan's life at this difficult time, he finally had someone to talk to. He now had someone to understand him and someone who was eager to listen. He held so much sadness and grief inside of him for so many years. We tried to analyze just why Alan became immobilized and seemed helpless when it came to acting in his best interest. I was able to help him understand his motivations a little more, to gain confidence and self-respect, and to see things clearly for once in his life.

Ultimately, the court case ended and not to Alan's advantage as hoped. It took over two years for the legal struggle to finally be over—a painful experience to say the least. However, even in losing there is much satisfaction in knowing that we tried to get Peter to see what was right.

We continuously say to one another that none of it really matters. We have each other and that is what counts the most. We have erased the painful memories of the past, and we will move on. We will persevere and we will find joy in our lives every day. And that is exactly what we are doing. And Peter has to live with the fact that he has benefitted greatly at the expense of his loving stepfather.

4

Ann's Story

M<small>Y STORY IS SIMPLER</small> than Alan's, although I recognize that it has been one of constant searching—for fulfillment, validation, and complete consuming love. Alan too was searching for love, but his path had so many more twists in it. I felt that I was happy at various times, but as I look back on my life I understand now that I was never truly at peace; nor was Alan.

When I broke it off with Alan at the end of 1961, I merrily returned to Cortland to see what awaited me there. Prior to returning home for that Christmas vacation I had had a date with an upperclassman and I have to admit that my head was kind of turned around. It certainly wasn't the reason that I broke things off with Alan, but it did trigger some thoughts about wanting to experience more. Although I had a few other dates with this fellow, it turned out that he was on and off-campus during the next three and a half years and continued to kind of drive me crazy by being inconsistent. I had been smitten, but it never amounted to anything; and even though I dated a lot, I never had a real boyfriend during my years at Cortland. In those days girls went off to college and expected to have a ring on their finger by the time they graduated. I soon understood that that was not going to be me, nor was that my ultimate goal or intention. I realized I wanted more than that—a career, maybe.

There was also something else that happened to me that should be told here because I now know that it had a huge effect on how I related to men and on what I ultimately was looking for in a relationship. It was a secret I kept for a very long time.

I mentioned earlier that my family made lifelong friends with people we met at Sugar Maples. We became great friends with a couple from New York City. He was a stockbroker on Wall Street and they lived in a penthouse apartment at Washington Square Village. My parents adored them, particularly my father. And they adored our little family. They were very good to us—consistently showering our family with attention and offering things that my parents could never afford—like taking us to restaurants in NYC all the time; upgrading our accommodations at Sugar Maples; introducing my sister and I to Broadway plays; and Rene even secured for me my first summer job at her company in the city. All of that started, for the most part, the summer before my senior year of high school. Through it all I was blind to see what was really happening. Ray was a tall imposing man who engaged everyone with his personality, his wealth, and his fun-loving demeanor. He was a charmer. He could tell stories and jokes like no one else and he was certainly someone to reckon with. They were both very influential in our family's life. So how shocked was I to receive a letter from Ray when we were still at Sugar Maples that summer. In it he told me he was *in love with me*! Ray had to be in his mid-fifties then and I wasn't yet 18. My sister, then 14, was with me when I picked up the letter and she wanted to know what it was all about. I was, of course, very shaken and couldn't believe what I was reading and I wasn't quite sure how to react. At first I thought that it was all a joke, but I soon realized that he was serious. What to do? How to react? What to think? I had no idea. I didn't say or do anything and I hid the letter. When we got home more letters came, expressing the same sentiments. Rene and Ray continued to visit our house and as he entered he would whisper to me that he was a nervous wreck and was having a hard time with it all. I did not know what to do. I remember going out to dinner with them on my 18th birthday and dancing with Ray. It was a very uncomfortable time. I was flattered, but in a way that I absolutely did not know how to deal with. How could this sophisticated man with an absolutely fabulous wife, want *me*? The letters continued and afternoon phone calls began. I still didn't know what to do or what to say, but I knew it couldn't continue. I hid the letters in my underwear drawer in the room that I shared with my sister.

One day it did come to an abrupt end.

I was at work at my part time job at A.S.Beck shoe store in Getty Square when a phone call came for me from my mother. When I asked what was wrong, she said, "It's Ray." I thought that she meant that something had happened to him. But, "No," she told me, "I found the letters in your room and we need to talk." She came to the store to pick me up and get me home. All she wanted to know was whether "anything had happened." I told her "no" and also told her that I was angry that she had intercepted the letters. And she told me, in no uncertain terms, that the whole thing must stop and no one was to say *anything* about it ever again. She said that Dad must never know. It would kill him. On the one hand, I was terrified and confused, and on the other, I was extremely thankful that my mother was the kind of woman she is and that she showed such strength to take it into her hands and help me find a way out. She told me that I was to phone Ray and tell him that it must end, and not to tell him that she knew. So, with her help, I was able to do just that: I told him that I couldn't handle it any longer; and that was it. My parents continued with the relationship and we continued to see them as we did before and my mother *never* let on that she knew. Only once did my mother and I ever mention it again to one another and I think that was after Ray passed away. To this day, I marvel at her strength. She knew what she had to do. She protected my father because she knew that he would be shattered if he knew that his wonderful friend had compromised his daughter in any way whatsoever.

I kept the secret too. I never told anyone. But I knew that it had affected me. First of all, it affected me because I became aware of the fact that I was attractive and desirable to a very sophisticated, elegant older man. And, secondly, it certainly had an impact on who and what I was attracted to. I know that I always made comparisons and for the longest time no one ever measured up. I did finally tell my sister and my best friend, Kathy, but that was much later after I was divorced. And, of course, I shared the entire story with Alan after we reconnected. And the remarkable thing about it all, is that it happened when Alan and I were coming together as a couple. I know that I was relieved when I started dating him so that I could disengage from the messy situation I found myself in and I was genuinely grateful for his attention. And, I do believe, that it perhaps might have had an impact on my breaking up with Alan too. In fact, we were at Rene and Ray's penthouse that Christmas vacation after I had told Alan I wanted to date others and my sister remembers that we were outside talking on their terrace and she could see that we were having a serious discussion. Who knows what it meant then? What I do know is that it had an impact on my life, even if I kept it in the deepest recesses of my mind for most of my life. Whether or not I felt at the time that I was searching for more, it is incredible to understand now that I have everything I ever needed or wanted in a man in Alan. He is my knight in shining armor.

Following graduation from Cortland, I secured my first teaching job in Highland Falls, New York, near West Point. The ironic thing about that event is that prior to the start of the school year, the day I was leaving home to move into my new apartment, Alan paid a visit to my parents' house in Hartsdale, and *he* was the one who packed me up in his car, drove me up to Highland Falls, and helped me to move in.

I taught 7th and 8th grade English and I was soon dating the 7th and 8th grade science teacher and assistant football coach. I was also considered somewhat of a home wrecker because he had been dating the girls' Phys Ed teacher before I arrived on the scene and they were supposed to be married. It was a fun year for me. Jim and I went back and forth each weekend to Westchester to either his home in Croton-on-Hudson or my home in Hartsdale.

I had a serious car accident that winter and I relied on Jim for many things after the accident while my broken arm was in a cast. Soon we were *sort of* engaged. At least that's what I told my parents. However, it soon became very clear to me that this was not going to be a lasting relationship, nor was he the man that I wanted to marry. I didn't see myself as the wife of the football coach and the life that would bring.

At the end of that one year I was recruited by the Briarcliff school system (the system that didn't hire me the year before) and I moved back home for a while until I rented an apartment in Ossining, New York. I spent three pleasant years there teaching 7th grade English, coaching the cheerleading squad, and socializing with the other young people on the faculty. I dated, but there was no one who struck my fancy.

It was the summer of 1967 when I was teaching at Briarcliff that my college roommate, Ann Hull, and I (we were known as the two Anns: Ann 1 and Ann 2) took our first trip to Europe. At that time teachers could get a round trip ticket to Europe for $239 and spend two entire months travelling through 12 different countries for the advertised "$5 A Day." It was a fabulous trip. We had a ball. We saw a lot; laughed a lot; and had many "entertaining" experiences in each country we visited. I even purchased a red Karmann Ghia convertible that we picked up in Frankfurt, Germany, in which we tooled around the continent, and then shipped back to the states. Boy, did we feel like jetsetters! It was during that fabulous, once-in-a-lifetime trip that I visited my Italian relatives in Torino, Italy, for the first time and started a wonderful relationship with cousin Piera (more on that in the chapter on Italy). Ann and I still remember the most intricate details of that trip and to this day we reminisce and laugh about all the fun and crazy experiences we had.

I remained a teacher for only four years. I soon realized that this was not going to be the ultimate career choice for me. I enjoyed my students immensely and I formed some very close bonds with them (in fact, I continued to see several of them after I was married and living in Massachusetts and have now connected with a few others on Facebook too). But the day-to-day curriculum planning and endless paperwork did not excite me. So I began researching other avenues and interviewing at publishing houses in New York City. It was at that time that Ann and I decided to take an apartment in Manhattan and we moved into a brand new building at the corner of 83rd Street and 1st Avenue. We both reverse-commuted to our teaching jobs, Ann on Long Island, and me in Briarcliff. We had a grand old time and I soon landed a job with Houghton Mifflin Company as an educational consultant—an elementary math consultant. Now I knew nothing about teaching elementary math, but I liked the idea of travelling and working with teachers to help them in their classrooms. I was good at that and I liked it, but the constant travel wasn't always as glamorous as it seemed to be at first.

At the same time I had an active social life in New York City, dating many interesting guys, while spending summer weekends in the Hamptons, and ski weekends during the winter in Vermont. It was the era of young singles pooling resources to rent houses together in such desirable locations. How cool were we?

Ann got married. My younger sister got married and most of my friends got married. It was at that time that I met a Scotsman at my friend Corinne's wedding and started a bit of travelling back and forth across "the pond," and for a while I really thought that I was going to marry him. I was the last hold-out, and it even looked like I might not be the marrying kind at all. It didn't bother me. I was not desperate to marry; far from it. I was having a great time being free, and I certainly hadn't found the guy who would shake my world. Was it that no one quite measured up to my ideal of a man? My career was fun and I even decided to move out of the city and take an apartment in Mt. Tremper, New York, near the famed Woodstock. It was the beginning of my semi-hippy days—even though I had a well-paying job and lived in a nice house. But I knew even then that I was also searching—searching for something more.

So that brings me to July 5th, 1971, when I travelled to Boston for an editorial meeting for the new textbooks for which I would be consulting. It is then that I met Keith (Kit), and by October we were engaged. Now I have to admit that there were no bells and whistles. There were no fireworks. It just seemed that we were in the right place at the right time and we seemed to fit. We were the exact same age (born within four days of one another); he was a lawyer (I certainly had determined by then that, if indeed, I did marry it would be to a professional man); he was of Italian descent; and he came from a similar background, or so I thought. (The house that he grew up in looked almost *exactly* like the Morsemere Avenue house that I grew up in). Outwardly, it all looked right and we seemed to get along and enjoy one another. But I was soon to realize that his background and his family were very different from mine and he had lots of baggage that he continued to deal with and would deal with forever. Kit had had a terrible relationship with his father who had died when Kit was nineteen years old. He never ever spoke with me about how he felt on that subject, but I knew that it had affected him greatly. I also was quite aware that it would be impossible to change Kit, but I felt that I would love him and help him deal with his "demons." At the time we decided to marry, he purchased a house in Cohasset, Massachusetts, a fourteen room house on five acres of land located on the inlet to Cohasset Harbor. It was here that we spent seven years of our lives and where our children were born.

The first three years of our marriage were actually quite lovely. We worked on our big beautiful house, we visited foreign lands, we had friends, and we were happy. All the while I was still working with Houghton Mifflin and travelling every week—until getting snowbound in Caribou, Maine, for an entire weekend, that is. That was it. I needed to stay closer to home and asked Houghton whether my travel could be confined to day trips from then on. It was no way to start a new marriage—being away all week.

During that three-year period I remember thinking that perhaps I didn't want to have children; perhaps this life was good enough for me. I don't know what snapped inside of me, but I soon realized that I desperately wanted to have children. As a couple, our desire to be parents became paramount in our minds. After all, I was 31 years old. Today, that seems so young to me, but in those days, I was old. I had been attending graduate school getting my master's at Lesley University and also started a doctorate at Boston College. I was going to go to England that August to study the English Infant Schools, but I changed my mind at the last minute and that is when David was conceived. I gave birth to him in May of 1975.

I was 32. I was blissfully happy. Being a mother consumed me. I loved it. However, I was given an opportunity to teach some courses at Bridgewater State College in elementary education when David was only four months old. I only taught two days a week and it all seemed to be working. When David was five months old, I became pregnant with Leigh and she was born on July 6, 1976. They were just fourteen months apart, but I loved it. I was very happy with my life as a mother, and for a whole year I was a mother only—no work. I remember driving in the back seat of my parents' car (they had come to pick me up and bring me and the children down to Hartsdale for a visit) with my two babies and feeling utterly content; nothing at all could bother me. In fact, my father remarked to me, "Annie, you don't get upset about anything any more!" This evidently was quite a change from my usual, more hyper personality.

After the children were born, Kit and I began spending more and more time apart. I was content to be at home with my children and working (I only spent one full year out of the workforce) and he was content to be in town at his office or with other friends socializing without me.

It is here that I must interject a fundamental truth. My two children, David and Leigh, are my raison d'etre. I cannot imagine my life without them. They are wonderful people and superior human beings. So I am grateful that my marriage to Keith resulted in giving life to them. David is a talented musician, a percussionist, living in Manhattan, consumed by music and competent in every genre, whether it be playing drum set in a rock and roll band or playing tympani with a symphonic orchestra. He performs brilliantly on all percussion instruments, composes music, arranges music—the whole nine yards. I am exceedingly proud of his accomplishments and am constantly in awe of his commitment to his craft. Leigh is a talented writer and publicist in the food and restaurant industry living and working in Italy and promoting the food and wine of the region of Puglia. She has taken remarkable risks in her work life, has excelled at every turn, and is highly regarded in her field. She is now embarking on a new venture: her ultimate goal of establishing her own business as a wellness coach and personal cartographer, offering wellness retreats in Italy and working with clients in the states. I am so proud of her achievements too. I love both of my children so very much and take pride in who they are and what their lives are all about.

Alan and I often say that we can never imagine life without our children. We are blessed that we have them and we love them. Steve has said that he wished Alan and I would have married long ago, so that he would have had me as his mommy all along. However, I reminded him, "Steve, you wouldn't have existed if we married back then!" Oh, yeah, how true. We talk about the fact that our mission now is to bring this blended family together, giving Steve and Joey (and hopefully Cheryl too, one day) the loving environment that they did not enjoy growing up. And David and Leigh can enjoy a bigger happy family as well.

Kit and I remained in the Cohasset house for the first seven years of our marriage. We continued to take trips. Kit insisted that we take a trip each year without our children. In fact, when David was just eight months old and I was three months pregnant with Leigh, we went to Jamaica for a week. It was a very difficult thing for me to leave my baby, but Kit's theory was that it would be extremely important that we have our alone time together at least once a year. So we took a similar trip to the Caribbean each year thereafter. In fact, I remember how utterly shattered I felt when the following year (David was 21 months old and Leigh was only 7 months old), we left them with our sisters (David stayed with my sister and Leigh stayed with Kit's sister). During the trip Leigh became sick and I didn't learn of that until we got home. I felt *horrible* that I had left them. I never fully agreed with Kit's insistence on taking those trips and I realized later that this was just one way in which he controlled me; how my own thoughts were negated and minimized throughout my marriage. Our trips also became the only time that we were intimate as the years wore on after the children were born. In retrospect I wonder if our situation was an example of how some men feel jealous after children are born and require some time with their spouse when attention can be placed completely on them again.

When we were together as a family everything seemed fine and Kit did little drinking on the weekends. Outwardly he seemed to be totally the family man; but in reality that was on the weekends only. During the week when he was in Boston at his law office and with friends, he lived in his own world that I was not to be a part of, while I ran the household and took care of the children alone. I remember once being told that I was *never* to appear unannounced at his office. So what was going on that I couldn't know about? I guess I will never know. Even after it was apparent that our marriage was over, and we started with divorce proceedings, I never learned the truth about all of that uncomfortable time and mysterious goings-on in his other life.

I now realize that our life together was not normal. It was not a loving family unit, although that is the way it appeared to others. Kit was a lawyer, of course, but an unconventional one. He would usually sleep until about 10 AM every day (after I had arisen by 6 and gotten the children off to school and myself off to work) and go to his law office. Even in those days (before casual days at work) he wore jeans to the office. And during the week he sometimes would not come home until three or four in the morning, or sometimes he wasn't even home by 6 AM (but always before the children awoke). I, on the other hand, would have been up all night waiting and worrying and then be a basket case at work the next day. I did all of the household chores—always—including taking out the garbage, as well as everything pertaining to the children; i.e. doctor's appointments, back-to-school nights, etc. We didn't show affection toward one another and we rarely had sex. He was a weekend husband. And the elephant in the room was consistently his drinking problem—a problem that he was never able to confront or acknowledge; a problem that consequently resulted in a diagnosis of end stage liver disease—a very sad state of affairs for my children and the rest of his family; and for me too, since I can't quite get my head around the fact that his life was cut so short.

Keith Vincola passed away on February 21, 2013; such a sad ending to a life that should have been so different. After his diagnosis in November of 2012, the end came very fast—way too fast for any of us to fully comprehend. In retrospect, it is evident now that the disease had taken hold long ago and he actually started failing rapidly from the beginning of the winter of 2012. My daughter had been living in Italy but she was in the states for business-related events January through the beginning of March, 2012. Following that time at home she had a huge row with her father and they were not talking until she returned home the middle of October when she and the rest of the family discovered that he had been hospitalized and the decline had accelerated. We'd all like to believe that his negative behavior was a direct result of his disease as he continued to alienate those few people who still stood by him, including his family. Leigh essentially became his chief caregiver since my son was on tour with the musical "West Side Story" and not regularly available. Leigh and Kit's sister, Karen, tried to make his life as comfortable as possible as he deteriorated. At the end Leigh asked me to come to be with her and I remained in Boston until he passed. I was so glad that I did that—not only for my children, but for me too. I did see Kit while he was still somewhat responsive and I was able to talk with him. I believe that he recognized me, knew that I was there, and that I wanted to offer my support. It somehow enabled me to erase some of the bad memories and concentrate on the good times so long ago. My son managed to fly in from Madison, Wisconsin for 24 hours and said a final farewell to his father. And Leigh stood the watch. She is remarkable. There was no wake or funeral at the time of his passing—instead a celebration of his life was held in April.

After our children were through the infant and toddler stages, our marriage changed and we continued to grow apart. On the surface, Kit seemed to be the model husband and father, but his stimulus and enjoyment really came from outside the house—with bartenders around town and his druggie friends, and a life-style that I couldn't deal with. Kit was basically a good person, but as he stated to his mother one time after our divorce, "I think I've been a good father, but I wasn't always a very good *husband*." I had to come to grips with the fact that we were miles apart in our values and how we viewed life.

During those early years after my children were born I soon realized that I had better have some outlets myself. I began working part time at several consulting jobs in Boston until I took a position as an Assistant Professor of Education at Stonehill College in North Easton, Massachusetts. At this time we decided to leave Cohasset and move to Brookline. In later years (and when we moved again from Brookline to

Boston after sixteen years in the Brookline house), I found myself saying that whenever we were having serious difficulties in our marriage, we moved. I think now that I would have been better off had I realized that at the time. Should I have left earlier? Probably. But I really couldn't. For one thing I couldn't afford to and then I was afraid of what Kit would do in terms of the children. I was afraid that he would take them away from me if I dared think about divorce. He was a very controlling individual.

We moved to Brookline in 1979 when David was four and Leigh was three. I was commuting to Stonehill for my job. David and Leigh were in care at the Pine Manor Child Study Center until about two in the afternoon. I did the driving to and from and any carpooling every day. I remember hiring a few of the students at the school to babysit for the children if I couldn't get back early enough. But sometimes I would come back from Stonehill and pick them up and then go back to the college (a 45 minute commute one way) and keep them with me until I was finished with my day. So I was struggling constantly to make it all work without any help from my partner, my husband. He was around it seemed when it counted and he provided us with a beautiful house and the money to do what we wanted; however, he took none of the responsibility of running the household. It was also the time that it looked like we had it all: a loving marriage, two beautiful children, a big beautiful house, dual careers. It was also the time in our lives that money was plentiful and so were the drugs. Smoking marijuana became a habitual activity from the beginning of our marriage, but it was during the '80s that cocaine was plentiful among our small circle of friends. I have to admit that I engaged in that activity myself and enjoyed the lifestyle to a degree, but not nearly as much as my husband did. It wore me out. And a few very stressful situations (when he was taking part in what I discovered to be some shady activity) convinced me that I wanted no part of it any longer.

It was at that time that I began researching and getting involved with employer supported child care. The movement was beginning in the United States and I was there at the start. Several other colleagues, whom I still hold in high esteem, had gotten involved and it interested me greatly. I decided to leave my position as Assistant Professor of Education at Stonehill College and start my own consulting firm. It was called Corporate Child Care Consultants. I started off with a bang and was fortunate enough to land an amazing contract with the Howard Johnson Company, then headquartered in Quincy, Massachusetts. I conducted a needs assessment and opened an on-site child care facility for infants through pre-school children for them at their brand new building. It was a great opportunity for me and I had made my mark. Following that, I was responsible for developing and opening the first child care facility in downtown Boston for Hill Holliday Advertising. That center was housed at the First Baptist Church, a block away from the Hancock Tower where Hill Holliday was located. This all happened in the early '80s. As a matter of fact, I was considered quite the child care expert at the time and was approached by executives from Bain and Company in Boston prior to their formation of the Bright Horizons

Corporation, currently the leading employer supported child care development company. One of the individuals who later became the CEO of the company sat in my living room and picked my brain about everything there was to know about the development of a child care center. I very naively shared way too much information. I always had a problem with that! I would find myself being forthcoming and helpful no matter what questions were asked of me. I never minded sharing my pioneering efforts with anyone who asked and certainly never got paid for that information. (The creation and development of Bright Horizons was one of the companies for which former Republican Presidential candidate Mitt Romney was responsible). Hmmm, should I have been less free with sharing that knowledge and expertise? You bet!

I continued working in the field for twenty years and formed several alliances and business partnerships along the way, until I was hired by Coopers & Lybrand (now Price Waterhouse Coopers) as their National Director of Work/Life Consulting in 1994. I was also one of the individuals responsible for starting the Alliance of Work/Life Professionals, the professional organization in our field. I published articles along the way, was interviewed periodically by the media, and made an excellent salary. I was proud of what I accomplished and I loved the work. After four years with Coopers & Lybrand in a high profile position, I was then recruited by two work and family vendor companies who offered me prestigious positions with ample compensation, which I accepted. However, it became apparent that the landscape started changing within the field that I had been instrumental in developing. The economy was beginning to change, too, and companies began looking at work/life benefits as add-ons that they could no longer afford. I felt uncomfortable with the changes that were occurring and felt that perhaps it was time to move on.

It was then that my divorce was imminent. I had known for about five years prior to finally deciding that we would divorce that our marriage was doomed. I had pleaded with Kit to go to marriage counseling with me, but he refused. As the children finished college and were out of the house and we moved into a five-story townhouse in the South End of Boston, we hardly had much to do with one another at all. I was constantly travelling with my job and Kit decided to take control of the renovation of our new home.

The breakup occurred over my father's birthday weekend. My mother and father had recently moved to Massachusetts from New York (close to my sister's house) when Dad needed to start kidney dialysis. David and Leigh were aware of our decision to divorce, but we had agreed (or so I thought) that we would not say anything while celebrating my father's birthday. After a rather tumultuous day at my sister's house the day after the birthday celebration (Mom and Dad were not present), it was announced (by Kit, violating our agreement) that we would be divorcing; making me very angry. The mess at my sister's house took place in July, but I didn't tell my parents until September. No one in our family had ever divorced before and I wasn't quite sure about the reaction I would get. I was pleased with what my parents had to say to me and I remember it clearly. Dad said, "Be smart and be careful." That was all. His health had already started to decline, but he was strong and supportive. And Mom said, "Why didn't you tell me? I'm your mother. I should have known you were unhappy." There was no question that they were both right there for me.

So that is when I found myself single again. I found myself making other life changes, too. I decided to leave my consulting work behind me.

I accomplished a lot during my consulting years. I was recognized nationally for the work I did and most of it was a very positive experience. I made some great friends as a result of my involvement and for that I am indeed grateful. However, I still felt that I didn't accomplish as much as I had wanted. Although I made, for what to me, was a huge salary during the late '90s, I didn't sell my company at a gigantic profit like some of my colleagues had, who were then set for life. I was never the shrewd business professional that would have enabled that. Once again, I felt that what I had accomplished fell short of what I had dreamed. Maybe that is why I kept changing direction and kept searching. That is what led to my purchase of Tisbury Antiques on Martha's Vineyard.

I have to say that I enjoyed the following ten years as a retailer and the owner of an antique and interiors business. I took a big plunge in 2004 and moved from the rental space I occupied on Main Street in Vineyard Haven and bought a building on State Road. It was a cute little house in the business zone. I was able to get a jumbo loan to buy the building since I didn't have a mortgage on my Vineyard home. It was well before the real estate collapse and, at the time, I felt that I was financially well-off, and my net worth was pretty substantial. And then in 2005, I purchased my house in Sarasota.

However, by 2007 everything started to change and real estate values started plummeting. I love the house and it is now where we are living full time, but it is not worth today what it was when I bought it.

I had determined almost a year before Alan and I reunited that I wanted out of the antique business, so I put that property on the market. It wasn't until June of 2010, after we were married, though, that I was finally able to sell the building and close the business. I don't miss it at all. I still own my house on the Vineyard, but we have decided to put it on the market too. It is a lot of work and expensive to keep up. Alan has been so helpful with all of the work that moving a business and maintaining an older property entails. He has done so much. He is so incredible, although he consistently says, "We are a team!"

Even though my career and my work were always very important to me, I know that I was continuously searching. I longed for someone to love me completely and unconditionally. I knew that I had never had that. After my divorce I joined Match.com. I soon met Peter, a sophisticated and well-travelled management consultant and former professional rugby player from Great Britain. Peter lived in Manchester, England, and we began a long distance relationship that lasted for several years. He wished me well on my new marriage. I dated others, but never seemed to find "the one."

I had gotten to a point that it really didn't matter to me if I found someone with whom I could share my life. I had great friends. I travelled internationally, as well as my back-and-forth trips from the Vineyard to Sarasota, and I was happy.

I had found myself again. I liked me and I liked my life. So I stopped searching for a mate and I let go.

And that is when Alan came back into my life.

PART TWO

Our Present

5

Becoming Best Friends Again

*I*T ALL STARTED on March 21, 2009.

I was at my house in Sarasota, Florida just killing some time and poking around on the Internet. Ironically, two days before that I had been doing the same thing and I began looking for friends on Facebook—something I had never done before. I had been on FB for two years already, having signed on mainly to keep track of my kids and see pictures of my sister's grandkids. I never included a profile. On that day I thought about looking up some high school and college friends and entered both school names. At the time it was a little early on for people of our age to be playing around with social media and few of us were on FB, so I was really ahead of my time. In fact, one of my niece's had said, "Wow, how cool are you Annie! You're on Facebook!" I didn't find *anyone* from either school and I went on to other things. So, when, two days later, I got a message and a friend request from Alan S. Votta, I was rather startled. And, apparently, so was he.

Alan was introduced to Facebook by his daughter-in-law, Catherine. Concerned about her father-in-law's happiness she said to him, "Dad, you're always doing something for everyone else. Why don't you do something for yourself for once? I'm going to teach you how to go onto Facebook. Maybe you can reunite with some of your old submarine buddies and add some color and interest to your life." At the time Alan was relatively new to the Internet and didn't know anything at all about Facebook.

Together Catherine and Alan developed a full profile for him, which, of course, included the name of his high school. Since I had been on there just two days earlier and had inserted Gorton '61 as my high school, the *only* name that popped up for Alan was one 'Ann Patavino Vincola'. Oh, and by the way, just before I logged off that day, while poking around, I decided to include my maiden name.

As Alan retells it, he was so shocked that he had to stand up and walk around the room and try to calm himself. You see, unbeknownst to me (or probably to him at the time) he had never forgotten me, and *everything* started flooding back into his mind. After a bit of reminiscing, he determined that he needed to send a friend request and a message to me. The message I got was: "Are you the same Ann Patavino that I went to Charles E. Gorton High School with? If so, a big hello from me."

I hadn't given Alan S. Votta a single thought during all those years from 1961 to 2009. I had gotten to a point where I felt that I was quite happy with my life and didn't think that a man or another relationship was in the cards for me. When I got the message from Alan I just felt a pleasant warm feeling engulf me and nothing else. But it was nice to see his name on my screen. My response to him was, "Oh, my gosh, and a big hello back. Of course it's me. What a wonderful surprise. Hope you are well. Ann." That message—those very words—Alan wrote on an index card that he carried around in his wallet for a year until our wedding in March of 2010.

After a few more introductory messages on that day, the ball started rolling—quickly, very quickly. Alan told me that he lived in Charleston, South Carolina; that his wife had passed away two years prior; that he had retired from the U.S. Submarine Navy; that he had four children and seven grandchildren; that he and his wife had built several successful businesses in the past; and that he was *really* glad to have found me. I told him that I was living in Sarasota and on Martha's Vineyard, that I owned an antique business on the Vineyard, that I had two children, and that I had divorced in 2000.

As soon as Alan read that, something snapped inside of him. He realized very quickly that he had never forgotten me, that he never lost the feelings he had had so long ago when we were 18 years old. He determined then and there that he was *not* going to let me slip through his fingers again. It took only two days and several back-and-forth messages to get to the point where he revealed his feelings. "These are the facts. When you broke off with me, the lights went dim, they never went out completely...."

Within two days of contacting one another, Alan was spouting words of undying love and I was apparently very receptive to it. We still talk about "How did this *happen?*" And that is where, we believe, Divine Intervention comes in. There is no other way to look at it. We are both very lapsed Catholics and not very religious at all, but we have learned to pray again and we have learned to thank God for what we have and what we have found in one another. We also feel that there are several people in heaven who are and have been cheering us on along the way, particularly Alan's mother, my father, and a few special old friends who have passed on. Tears often well up in our eyes when we think about this and know that the bleachers are full up there in heaven with our very special cheering squad.

There is no question in Alan's mind that he never lost the love that he had for me from our high school days and once we reunited he was able to act upon those feelings that lay dormant for all those years. I, on the other hand, continued to be rather cautious and incredulous at the beginning. But there was no question that I was very receptive to learning about his feelings and wanted to hear more. We both had an incredible need and desire to be loved fully and completely and longed for that soul mate to appear in our lives. Who knew that we would find that in one another?

Two books have had a great impact on us along the way (and we included references to both in our wedding ceremony). One of those was *When God Winks* by SQuire Rushnell. Now SQuire is a Vineyarder, and he and his wife, Louise Duarte, have become friends of ours. SQuire's premise (he has written several other books, with his newest entitled *DivineAlignment*) is that nothing in our lives happens in isolation—there are no coincidences—and God has a hand in making them happen; thus, they are "God Winks."

Alan and I know that we have experienced one God Wink after another and we continue to. We have also found that there were so many things over the years (when we didn't have a clue about what was happening in one another's lives) that we now recognize as God Winks: we both were in the antique/interior design business; we both had two hips replaced (almost within the same time frame); we both smoked Benson & Hedges cigarettes (when we smoked long ago); we both drove Nissans; our tastes are so alike in music and other entertainment; and the list goes on and on. And most incredible of all, Alan had discovered the silver ID bracelet that I had given him in 1961 in his old jewelry box (the contents of which had mostly disappeared or changed many times over during the intervening fifty years) and he had started wearing it again just two months before we were in contact with one another. It was the only thing from that jewelry box that went back to that era. Therefore, we continuously speak about God Winks and we know that they have played a huge part in this story. The other book is Kahlil Gibran's *The Prophet*. Alan began quoting from *The Prophet* in his emails as Gibran's words came to life for him over and over again.

As we began on this road of reconnecting and becoming best friends again, there was much to learn about what had transpired in one another's lives, especially in Alan's world.

I was so happy to know that he had kept his values and integrity in place no matter what obstacles stood in the way. It made me realize all the more what an incredible individual he is and how lucky I am to have been given a second chance to have him in my life.

Catherine, the Facebook liaison, and her husband, Alan's son Steve, have continued to figure very importantly in our lives on a daily basis. We love them both very much, and love their two amazing boys, Max and Stephen.

There were several emails between Catherine and I during this time of being reintroduced to one another too. Her short, but very revealing emails to me began to paint a picture—a picture that would continue to become clearer and clearer to me. In one of her first emails after I had asked whether she could help Dad get some pictures up on FB, she said,

> *Hi Ann! I am so glad Dad has renewed his friend-ship with you. The women in his life that I know about have been horrendous to the point that I am surprised he wants anything to do with any females! He has such fond memories of his days growing up in Yonkers. And yes, I will be glad to take some pics of him and get them posted. Catherine*

That was my first clue that Alan had a lot more to tell me than he had first revealed. As Catherine worked on getting some pictures posted of her father-in-law, so that I could get a sense of just what Alan looked like after 48 years, I received another email from her that told me even more.

Hi! I created an album with a few pics of Dad. Unfortunately we don't have many because for years (seven to be exact) we weren't allowed over at their house because of The Evil One (Steve's stepmom). Anyway, that's another story. We'll get some new ones soon! Catherine

It became obvious that Alan and I were going to be getting together soon and I would be meeting this family. That email was followed by:

Can't wait, would love to meet you! You have brought a new happiness into his life. We love him so much. He is such a sweetheart. Cat

But it wasn't until the plans for our engagement party got underway that I was to hear more about the family and the schisms that existed. Amy, Peter's wife, had determined that she was going to host a party at their farm. The affair was taken out of Catherine's hands completely and Amy was in charge of my introduction to the family at a party in our honor. Catherine then sent me two emails that described Steve's struggle and conflict about whether he would attend the event. Catherine continued to communicate with me in an upbeat manner and looked forward to our meeting. And then I received this email:

Hi Ann! I don't even know where to begin—a phone call is probably in order I guess. I don't know what you know about Steve's relationship with Peter. I'm sure by now you at least know it is strained at best. It seems really important to Dad that we be at the party Amy is throwing for you two. Therein lies the problem. While the boys and I are planning on going, Steve is adamant about not going. As much as Dad would like Steve to just set aside his feelings, it is just not that simple. I think if the party were held at a neutral place it would be fine, but it is fair to say that flaunting what Peter has (that was given to him as with everything else in his life) just brings up bitterness and resentment in Steve and to a lesser degree in Joey. You have to understand that when Alan married Demi, Peter got an awesome dad but Joey and Steve got less than zero, in both love and material things. They both have worked so hard to achieve what they have. They grew up in a household where they were reminded constantly that they were the "guests" in Demi's house and to remember that. While Steve loves his Dad fiercely, he just does not feel compelled to have to include Peter in our lives. He understands that Dad loves Peter, but that doesn't mean he should be forced to hang around with him. The fact that Peter still, even at almost 40, refuses to see the inequities of the past and criticized him so harshly for not feeling remorse at Demi's death has fueled the resentment. Soooooooo…welcome to the family! Sorry we are such a mess! However, I love my husband deeply and, of course, will support him on this. I just wanted you to know it has absolutely

*nothing to do with you! He is so happy that his dad
has a chance to see what a real marriage is like and to
have someone love and APPRECIATE him for the
incredible person he is. We look forward to getting to
know you! Love, Catherine*

So, I was getting the picture about the family dynamics
that weren't all that pleasant, but the relationship between Alan
and I moved on nevertheless. These early emails will give you
a peek at how quickly sentiments were revealed. After Alan
sent his first email and friend request, and I responded, it
was still early in the morning of the first day of contact. This
followed shortly after:

*Of course only if you are the "Ann Patavino"—Fact
is, you remain in a special place in my memories and
my friendships—Sugar Maples and Sleigh Riding....
ALAN "Forever Your Friend"*

By that evening Alan laid out what his life was all about,
and then added:

*Lots more to talk about. Are you in contact with any
of the old Gorton crowd?
I think that is enough for now but I am excited
to hear from you!!! What about my little "Sister
Emma"?....FOR NOW
ALAN XXX"*

And after I told Alan about my current status, that I was single and available, the following two emails were sent within twenty-four hours of one another.

Annie, I am finding it so hard to think and compose any words that would or could make any sense right now. However, This is for sure…. "Thanks For The Memories"

More Then A Friend ALAN XXX

Dear Annie, I fear, I have opened "Pandora's Box." Many thoughts and feelings have come alive after many years lying dormant in my psyche and my heart.

Because of many reasons presently I can't act on what my heart is telling me to. These are the facts; the short time we were together—was the best time of my life! When it came to an abrupt end, I felt like a ship without a rudder. Tears in my eyes are giving me away. I have been in love with you since our first date, through the break up and for the next 50 years. Sounds foolish but it is as true as true could be. Do you remember the first day of 7th grade? I followed you all the way to your home that afternoon. When you went inside I very bravely approached the front steps, leaned over, touched the steps and told myself I'd be back! Took 5 years but I made it! You were wearing a charcoal gray skirt with a bib front with two broad straps over your shoulders and a white blouse. At this point I hope I have not offended you. If I have, well that is how it has to be…50 years of holding it deep inside. Feels like a ton of bricks have come off my heart. Sorry I have messed up our pen pal reunion.

Remember? "If I Did Not Love You The Ink Would Never Leave This Pen"—I put that in every letter I wrote to you while you were at Cortland State.…With All Of My Deepest Love ALAN

XXX XX X

The last email blew me away. Not only because he admitted that he loved me then and still felt the same way, but that he remembered what I wore that first day of school when we entered the 7th grade! The amazing thing is that I made that outfit. And he remembered it *exactly*. It was my great accomplishment prior to beginning 7th grade and a new school. There is a picture of me in that outfit in the Gorton 1957 yearbook. I was the Secretary of the 7th grade class and I was in a picture of 7th, 8th, and 9th grade officers and there I was with the outfit on.

That evening we spoke on the phone for the first time and remained on the phone for over three hours. On the 24th of March, just three days after we started communicating, this is some of what I sent back to Alan:

I had a very restless night and couldn't think of anything else but our conversation. There is so much emotion coming out of me that I really don't know how to react or think. But one thing is for sure, I am not in the least bit uncomfortable about what you are saying so have no fear about that. A little incredulous, yes, but uncomfortable, no. It was so very wonderful talking with you last night. It felt comfortable and natural and peaceful at the same time.

My horoscope has been telling me that 2009 is to be a banner year for me in all ways (one that only comes along every 12 years or so) and that I was going to really fall in love as well. Who would have ever thought it could be YOU!!!!! Not me. I have to honestly say that I have not thought about you and wouldn't think that there was any hope of anything being rekindled. When I move on, I really move ON!

I am thrilled that you are feeling the way you do, but I also go forward with caution. I am definitely not the 18 year old that you loved back in 1961, but I hope that the qualities that you loved back then will still be evident. It will be quite incredible once we do meet again. As I said to you, I feel that although I have been very happy, something has always been missing. I have missed the feeling of warmth and bliss and real comfort with a partner. So thank you from the bottom of my heart for feeling the way you do and let us just see where this takes us. Love, Ann

Alan's response:

My Dearest Darling Ann, WOW!! The flood gates are officially open. This contact has me so shook up! I welled up before but now I am crying like a baby.

So, so much to digest and fully comprehend. Every sensory fiber in my body is on overload. I am in a state of total bliss. I feel like I can fly or solve the problems of the world. I am so totally tuned into ecstacy I can burst. My Dearest Darling Ann—I Love You even more than I did before—Ann Patavino, I Love You To Infinity and Beyond!!!

Dear GOD, thank you for allowing me to experience this gift you call love. I will honor this gift and cherish it for the rest our lives. My ANN, I LOVE YOU IN A PURE AND UNADULTERATED WAY. I LOVE YOU AS IT WAS INTENDED. I LOVE YOU, MY ANN. IT SOUNDS SO GOOD... With All Of My Deepest Love,

ALAN (W/CAUTION) XXX XX X OOOO

While lying in bed, it dawned on me. I always called you Ann and not Annie. Our friends called us Annie and Al, but between you and I, it was always Ann and Alan.

My Dearest Darling Ann, my every thought since last we spoke has been about you. It has been a lifetime since I experienced anything like this and I am LOVING EVERY NANO SECOND OF IT. My hope is that we both have a deep down gushy, I mean down to our marrow, gushy loving, exhilarating, experience of a lifetime. Ann, my Ann, I Love You. I Love You with all of my being, with all of my heart and soul!

My heart will not let me stop. A few short days
ago I was awoken out of deep hibernation.
With All Of My Deepest Love ALAN XXX XX X
ooooooooooooooooooo

That is just one example of the hundreds of emails that followed. Alan was amazing in revealing his feelings. We still talk about that every day and I question him on it. I ask him, "How are you able to express those feelings so well?" He does that now with friends and relatives as easily as he was able to tell me how he felt then. In writing all of these emails Alan says that he was driven by some other source. He just wrote and wrote. He was up at all hours of the night. Couldn't sleep at all. And he just kept writing. When we read over the emails now, he still feels that he was somehow guided in the writing. He says, "Where did those words come from?" He is amazed at his ability to pen his thoughts so well.

Alan had never been motivated, nor did he ever have the opportunity to reveal his innermost feelings to anyone before, but he hoped that one day he might be able to. He was finally aware that during his previous marriages his partner didn't care about what he thought or felt. He now realized his search ended with the woman he loved deep down inside for all these many years—me. Although this thrilled him immensely, he was also concerned that he might be moving too fast and making me feel uncomfortable. For that reason I sent this email to him one week after we started communicating:

I have to say that I am in no way turned off by your statements, nor do I feel anything negative…that you are pushing me too fast, etc. In fact, I am learning to look forward to hearing more. But being the realistic and cautious woman that I am, I still have these little gnawing feelings…what if our expectations of one another are not met? And I mean that for both of us. You say that this experience has been incredible for you and that your feelings won't change. It has been SIX DAYS since we have been in contact with one another and 48 YEARS have passed by!!!! I do feel that the man you are today is a more mature and "seasoned" individual but with the same wonderful qualities that made you a unique individual at 18.

And so it continued and moved on. The emails came fast and furiously—sometimes three or four a day. We then began speaking on the phone each day; sometimes two or three times. Then the flowers started—and the little gifts. It became necessary for me to fly up to Massachusetts to make arrangements for my mother to move into assisted living. She had been in an independent apartment in Springfield, Massachusetts, but then required more attention and care. Alan was wonderful through that and helped me a lot. He had also begun to send notes and flowers to Mom too, which delighted her no end.

We continued on this amazing coming together. But it was getting impossible to schedule that first face-to-face meeting until I was back up north and was at my house on Martha's Vineyard.

6

Telling Life Stories—
Establishing a Foundation
for a Lasting Relationship

So much was revealed in our emails back and forth between March 21st and the date of Alan's arrival at Logan Airport in Boston before we headed to my house on Martha's Vineyard. Although we had learned a lot about one another, we knew that we had to wait until our face-to-face meeting to understand where our lives had taken us and just what we had experienced. During those six weeks of emailing and talking, we had shared so much, written so much, talked so much. Therefore, we certainly felt very familiar with one another by then and intimate details had been revealed—not to mention the phone sex!

However, it was important to see if that chemistry was still there. A lot more talking, making love, and just feeling each other's presence was necessary. And Alan had some important details about his life to disclose. He waited until we were together to let me know about two of the life struggles that were an important part of his story. We had begun to feel so comfortable with one another even before seeing each other face-to-face that Alan decided that he would send a package of his clothes and personal items ahead of his arrival so that he would be unencumbered at the airport when we met.

He tells the story of the scene at the airport many times. He was so nervous that he thought he was at the wrong airport. On the other hand, I was perfectly calm and very relaxed. I left the island early that morning and stopped in Weymouth, Massachusetts, to see my sister-in-law, Donna, before heading to Logan Airport in Boston to pick up Alan. Donna had been suffering with lung cancer for over five years and she was starting to fail. Donna and I were very close. She was my ex's brother's wife. Although not divorced, they were not living together. Donna called us the "outlaws" of the family. I was able to talk with her about Alan and how I felt about seeing him again. (Alan eventually did meet Donna and they got on famously, as I knew they would. She even introduced him as her brother-in-law). Unfortunately Donna lost her fight with the cancer that had invaded her body and she passed away in May of 2010. I miss her very much.

From that first meeting at the airport, our time together was magical. Alan said that from the moment we laid eyes on one another and were locked in each other's arms, he knew that he had come home—after a long arduous journey. We travelled to the Vineyard in my car with me at the wheel. Alan sat in the passenger seat and couldn't stop looking at me and smiling for the entire trip to Woods Hole before we got onto the ferry. After we got to my house we sat for a while and that is when Alan revealed to me what happened with his daughter, Cheryl, and also about what he was dealing with as a result of Demi's will. Once again he cried in my arms, the second time in his life to do so. He had someone to listen to him again, to share his burden—the only person he was ever able to do that with—me. I listened and I sympathized. I felt his pain. It was the beginning of our journey to support one another and to understand those experiences that had a profound effect on our separate lives.

Before our first visit Alan had relayed to me a very special experience he'd had in his living room at his home in Charleston. He had been consumed with thoughts of me and obsessed with writing emails and speaking on the phone. He didn't sleep at night and he was often up at dawn sitting on his deck, looking out on the marsh, watching the sun rise, and thinking about what was happening in his life. One afternoon a feeling of complete exhaustion overcame him and he sat down on the recliner in his living room. He closed his eyes, but he didn't fall asleep. Resting in the middle of the day was highly unusual for Alan. As he sat there twilighting he heard his name being called. "Alan. Alan." He looked to his right and he saw his mother smiling at him. He looked to his left and she was still there. She kept calling him and he felt a warm feeling engulf him. At another point he looked straight ahead and there was my father. He, too, was smiling at Alan. Alan took it as a sign that they were giving him their approval that Alan and I had reunited. He was startled, but he was certain of the visions he had seen. The visions were definitely there for him.

Around that same point in time, I had had an experience of my own. I explained to Alan that I often felt disappointed that I didn't dream about my father or feel his presence at all. I was a little jealous that my sister did have dreams of my father. But I distinctly remember one day at the Vineyard, when I profoundly felt my father's presence. It was around the same time that Alan saw his visions. I do believe that my father was trying to tell both of us that he was very happy that we were back together again.

Alan also experienced another unexplained phenomenon. As he sat at his desk and composed his emails to me on the computer, he became distracted by a shadow that seemed to move around on the wall above and in front of him. Every time he looked up to focus on it, it would disappear. That happened over and over again—for two weeks—before his departure to visit me. Alan made a point of telling me about it. He couldn't understand what it was at the time.

Those two weeks that we spent at the Vineyard from May 12th till May 28th were very special. I loved being able to share the island with Alan, a place he had never been before. And I was so pleased that he was able to spend some time with two friends from the island who meant so much to me: my dear friends, Carol and Barbara. Those two figured into my life quite a lot during my years on the Vineyard.

Alan and I melded together very easily. And, of course, it was very nice to be able to make love without any encumbrances and to be able to experience the closeness that we didn't experience 50 years ago. I was very happy, but I still remained cautious and incredulous; in other words, not yet ready to commit or make any declarations. I also had to work at my store. So I would leave each day before eleven and get back to the house between five and six. In the meantime, Alan began repairing little things at my house. It was my introduction to having my "live-in handyman," and that was very nice indeed.

After Alan had been with me for about five days, he had a moment of uncertainty. He told me later that evening, when I returned home, that he had determined during that day he was going to leave…without telling me! He felt that he was putting pressure on me and that his very presence was interfering with my being able to think through where our relationship was going. He felt that if he left me to think, it would be better for both of us. In fact, he went upstairs to my attic to search for a suitcase in which he could pack his belongings (since he had sent his clothes and personal articles on ahead of his arrival). He planned to take the ferry, then visit my mom in Springfield, Massachusetts first, and then fly back to Charleston.

He couldn't find a suitcase in the attic, but instead he found a book of poems called *Leaves of Gold*. My friend, and college roommate, Ann, had given it to me after we took our trip to Europe and it was one book that I treasured. The book sat opened near my grandmother's old sewing machine, with sunlight beaming down on it through the small window in the attic. Alan felt compelled to pick up the book and started thumbing through it. A poem jumped out to him. The poem was called "Waiting" by John Burroughs.

Serene, I fold my hands and wait,
Nor care for wind, nor tide, nor sea:
I rave no more 'gainst time or fate,
For, lo! Mine own shall come to me.
I stay my haste, I make delays,
For what avails this eager pace?
I stand amid the eternal ways.
And what is mine shall know my face.

Asleep, awake, by night or day,
The friends I see are seeking me:
No wind can drive my bark astray,
Nor change the tide of destiny.

What matter if I stand alone?
I wait with joy the coming years:
My heart shall reap where it has sown,
And garner up its fruit of tears.

The waters know their own, and draw
The brook that springs in yonder heights:
So flows the good with equal law
Unto the soul of pure delights.

The stars come nightly to the sky:
The tidal wave comes to the sea:
Nor time, nor space, nor deep, nor high,
Can keep my own away from me.

He stood there and read the poem over and over. He went downstairs with the book and waited for me to get home. When I arrived home, he explained that he'd almost left the island that day. Then he told me all about the book and the poem. We sat there and read it together. I told Alan that I would have been devastated if he had left. I could certainly understand that he wanted more from me at the time, in terms of a commitment, but I just couldn't act that fast. He, on the other hand, had known from the very first email how he felt and that he wanted me by his side forever. We talked it out and he decided that he would be patient and let me have some time. He would be content "Waiting," but would remain with me until his scheduled departure after Memorial Day.

We continued to have a very special time. We went to my favorite places on the island; Alan met other island friends and acquaintances, and it was fun. Our plan then was to leave the island on the Friday before Memorial Day, go to Chatham on Cape Cod to visit our high school friend, Kathy, and then continue on to Springfield, and Wilbraham, to visit my mother and my sister and brother-in-law.

We left the Vineyard and arrived at our first stop, Chatham, on Cape Cod. My dearest and best friend, Kathy Scott, had lived on the Cape for many years. Kathy and I remained very close over the years, and when Alan re-entered my life, Kathy was ecstatic for me. She was very eager to see him too. She remembered the kind, wonderful guy he was in high school. Kathy and I had attended a Gorton reunion in 2001, when three classes got together: the classes of '59, '60, and '61. Driving to the Catskill resort where that reunion weekend was held, Kathy and I had visions of seeing our old boyfriends, Buzzy and Richie, from that year (my junior year) when we double-dated. Richie had been my first boyfriend and the person I went out with before my relationship with Alan. Richie was there at the reunion, but Buzz didn't attend. Nevertheless, we had a wonderful time and, subsequent to that, the four of us did get together on a few occasions in Florida and at the Vineyard. Kathy has suffered with some serious health issues over the past few years, so it became important for Alan and I to visit her. And she was equally eager to have the opportunity of seeing us together again.

We had a wonderful visit with Kathy, went out to dinner together, stayed overnight at her house, and laughed a lot. It was the first experience of many that would follow when we met up with old friends and family and shared the high that we were on. It was the first indication that the people who love us understood the very special thing that was happening. We would continue to feel that over and over again. Still it was early in the scheme of things and I remained cautious. It was not yet evident to us where it would lead, but I believe that the people we encountered along the way knew.

We left Kathy's home on Silver Leaf Lane (situated near the historical Chatham Light House) and started our drive to Springfield and Wilbraham, to finally visit with my mother and my sister. Alan had determined that he wanted to visit my father's grave at the Veteran's Cemetery in Agawam, Massachusetts beforehand. During the time that we spent at the Vineyard when we shared so much about our past lives, I told Alan that my ex-husband had never really proposed to me, nor did he ever ask my father for my hand in marriage. After all, we were 29 years old and he was a lawyer, and it was the early '70s. Being independent and forgoing traditional customs was our sophisticated approach—at least that was our thinking. In that respect, my father was denied the pleasure of being asked for my hand, and of walking his eldest daughter down the aisle. We opted for a simple wedding by a justice of the peace in a hotel room. Now, you need to know the kind of man that my father was to fully appreciate how disappointed he had been. He loved and respected all women and he totally adored his two daughters. And traditional values were very important to him. Alan understood this from the first time he met my father. So—upon hearing all of this Alan decided (unbeknownst to me) that he was going to speak to Dad at his graveside and tell him that one day soon he was going to ask for his permission to marry his daughter. That's why it was so important for Alan to get to the cemetery that day. (Later it was important for my son, David, to walk me down the aisle and represent my father.)

As we crossed the Bourne Bridge that day and traveled on Route 495, the skies opened up: it was a torrential downpour. It rained for the entire trip to Agawam. Miraculously, however, as we approached the gates to the Veteran's Cemetery, the sun came out. To our surprise, it hadn't rained there at all that morning. The weather had been terrible for days before that, and it had rained for some 45 consecutive days; thus, the grass hadn't been cut for some time. Arriving there under a blue sky, we had anticipated that the ground would still be wet and that we would need to walk through wet grass to Dad's grave. The grass wasn't wet at all. We approached Dad's grave:

Carmen A. Patavino
Tech 4, World War II
1911–2003

We stood holding one another. Alan found two stones, handed me one, and we kissed them and placed them on top of the tombstone. He explained to me it was an old Hebrew tradition to leave something behind from your visit to indicate that you had been there. (Alan had worked at a Jewish cemetery when he was a boy in Yonkers and knew of that custom.) Then Alan asked me to step back while he spoke to Dad. I could hear him say, "Carmen, I love your daughter very much and someday soon I want to ask her to marry me. And I very much want your permission and blessing to do so."

At that point Alan noticed something very important. Since it was Memorial Day Weekend there was a small flag placed at each graveside. And because the sun was shining, a shadow was cast on the ground as the flag waved in the breeze. Alan looked at it and he said to me, "Look at that! It is the same shadow that I saw on the wall at home when I was writing emails to you! I *knew* that it meant something! It was your father—telling me that he was there and that he approved." It was a sign. Another God Wink. Another indication that we were being watched and there was approval as to what was happening.

The incredible thing was that upon departing the cemetery, we immediately drove right back into the rainstorm that had miraculously disappeared as we had earlier approached the cemetery.

We left the cemetery and headed directly to Reed's Landing to see Mom. Alan had written to Mom and sent her flowers. She sent him a thank you note, which he's cherished. The note Mom wrote to Alan is probably the last of the kind that we will ever see. Here's what she said:

> *Dear Alan,*
>
> *How nice to hear from you, and it has made me very happy to know that you are back in my life and that you and Ann have renewed your friendship.*
>
> *I look forward to seeing you.*
>
> *Regards,*
>
> *Helen Patavino*

He was so eager to see her. And Mom was equally eager to see Alan. It was a wonderful visit. Mom remembered the last time she had seen Alan when he visited at the house in Hartsdale. Alan reminded her that he loved her Spanish rice. Mom told Alan that she was happy to welcome him back to the family, but she also told him that she wouldn't have recognized him if she passed him on the street. At almost 95 years of age, Mom consistently amazed us at some of the things she would say and how "right on" she was about most things. She certainly has memory lapses, and her short term memory isn't what it used to be, but on the big things she is right there. It was a beautiful moment for all of us. Having Mom as the last of our parents, Alan and I felt blessed that we were able to share our joy with her.

Then it was on to Meeting House Lane to see Emmie and Eddie. Alan couldn't wait to see Emmie after all these years, and I was equally anxious for Alan to meet Eddie, my brother-in-law. Eddie and I knew one another before he and my sister started dating at Cortland. Eddie joined the Marine Corps and they were married the week after Em graduated from Cortland in 1968. He was then sent overseas to what we thought was to be Vietnam, but he was deployed to Okinawa instead. Thank God. Em actually got pregnant the night before he left in January 1970 and their son, John (my godson), was born on August 13, 1970, when Eddie was still overseas.

When Eddie returned from Okinawa, they moved to Rochester, New York, and he began teaching elementary school. At the time, I was working at Houghton Mifflin as an educational consultant, and I was able to get Eddie an interview with my boss when we were doing a trade show in Syracuse. Eddie was offered a job as a salesman on the spot and he stayed with Houghton until his retirement.

There was another reason why I was so anxious for Alan and Eddie to meet. During the 27 years I was married to my first husband, Eddie and Kit had a somewhat odd relationship with one another. They appeared to be good friends and they went on camping trips, bringing John and David along. But there was always tension between them. Kit had a way of making others feel inadequate. As Eddie said, "Kit was high maintenance!" When we divorced there were definitely some struggles between my sister's family and me that were difficult to get through. You see, no one close to me knew how unhappy I had been or what my marriage was really like. I believe they thought that I was walking out, while the reverse was true. In what became an emotional scene at their house when I told them that Kit and I would be divorcing, Emmie said, "But we don't want you to." Eddie and I had some real "Come to Jesus" moments because he attempted to stand by Kit for a while, and some strong words were exchanged, but we got through that and finally became closer than ever. I was able to be honest with both of them and to reveal some truths that needed to be told; and they finally understood. They have been amazingly supportive of me from that time on.

Because of our past, I felt that it would be wonderful for Eddie and Alan to get along and become solid and fast friends. Of course, the fact that Eddie had been a Marine and Alan was a Navy man helped too. Alan called Eddie a jarhead, and Eddie teased him that he had spent too much time underwater. What fun we had together. When we arrived at their house, Em and Ed were sitting up at their beautiful pool. We walked through the house and Alan called out, "Where's my little seester?" They jumped into each other's arms, laughed and cried, and completely wiped away fifty years of separation. Her big brother was back in her life. And Alan and Eddie warmly embraced each other too. Alan said, "I hope no one takes a picture of me hugging this jarhead!"

We stayed there for three nights and we spent some quality time together. Eddie loves to cook and we were treated very well indeed. I specifically remember sitting around, talking and talking. Later on, when we visited again, at Christmas time, I overheard Eddie telling his sons that Alan "is a really good guy." So that weekend was important for all of us, and it became the foundation for a special bond.

The one very humorous situation of the weekend was Alan's teasing Eddie about the twin beds that we were forced to sleep on in my nephew Matt's old bedroom. Eddie refused to make changes in those rooms and get a *queen sized bed*! Two of the boys were married, with four children between them, and his daughters-in-law had tried to convince him to get a bigger bed. But it never happened. Eddie just wanted to keep things the way they always were when "his boys" were boys. Alan would constantly kid Eddie that he was going to secretly order a new bed and have it delivered to the house. So, every time we visit we are relegated to sleep in the twin beds and that is the *only* time that we are apart at night.

The twin beds played a big part in how that weekend at Em and Ed's house ended. Alan was to fly out from Boston on Monday morning to go back to Charleston. When he booked the flight, he really didn't pay attention to the fact that his flight was at 5:30 in the morning. When we focused on it, and realized that it would be virtually impossible to get to the airport in time, we had to get on the phone and change the reservation. It took a bit, but we were able to arrange a later departure that day.

When we awoke that morning Alan came over to my single bed and we cuddled together for a while. As we lay there talking, realizing that we were going to be saying goodbye later that afternoon, something came over me. Alan said that it was kind of weird and that I was acting rather strangely. I became very silent with my left hand on my head in a contemplative position. I didn't say anything for quite a while. What was going through my head? I know that I lay there facing Alan and thinking, "What am I waiting for?" I knew that he wanted to hear "I love you," but could I say it? I finally was able to think, "He's leaving here today. We have had such a wonderful time together. And, yes, I think I do love him! So why not just say it?" And that's exactly what I did. After what seemed to be an interminable amount of time to him, as I lay there with my hand on my head, I said, "I love you, Alan." Ah, what a moment. He was over the moon! He wanted to hear that so much. He felt like jumping out of bed and rushing downstairs to tell Emmie and Eddie that I had finally said it.

Thus ended our first weeks together. It was the start of such a miraculous series of events and a wonderful beginning to the rest of our lives. What followed was what we affectionately called our "victory tour." We were separated again for several weeks before Alan again travelled up north for another visit. Alan had to go back to his job at Home Depot and I needed to be at my store and get ready for the summer season.

Photographs

Ann and Alan,
Easter Sunday, 1960

Ann and Alan,
Sorority dance, 1960

Ann and Alan, Before the Prom, Morsemere Ave., 1961

Prom night at the Copa, NYC, 1961

Senior Prom, Pleasantville Country Club, 1961

Gorton YWCA girls' club, 1961

Ann on graduation night, GHS, 1961

Anne and Alexander Votta, 1993

Helen and Carmen Patavino, St. Augustine, FL., 1991

Engagement party, July 2009

Wedding party, March 13, 2010

Ann and Alan, wedding day, March 13, 2010

Ann and Alan, wedding reception

Gorton guys, wedding reception

My musician son, David Vincola

My daughter and food writer, Leigh Vincola, Puglia, Italy, 2011

Cousin Piera Fogliatto, Florence, Italy, 2010

Photographs

Alan's son Steve
and Catherine
Votta, 2011

Alan in Torino,
Italy, 2010

Don Piccolo, Brian Piccolo and Alan Votta, Coney Island, 1957

7

The Courtship and Engagement

ALAN WOOED ME. He said and did remarkable things that slowly and surely made me realize that this was special and that our life together would be sensational. The very first thing that Alan did, which remains so memorable to me, is that he sent me a Christmas card—in April, that is. I was still in Sarasota and it was well before we had our first face-to-face meeting. The card was a big Santa Claus with a lovely message, sending good wishes and holiday cheer. Inside, Alan wrote, "Every day is Christmas now that you are back in my life." I remember telling my friend Tammy about the card and she couldn't get over it. Her only comment was, "How romantic."

Alan continued to be sweet and generous and loving. He sent flowers to my house in Sarasota prior to when I flew up north to help Mom move into assisted living. He had mentioned on the phone that I should be expecting something to arrive soon. For a while I thought that *he* was going to show up at my doorstep. That was kind of unsettling to me because I wasn't ready to see him just yet. But, instead, the most beautiful vase of roses and irises, along with a small teddy bear (which he named Morsemere) arrived. I was delighted. The vase was the exact color of the walls in my sitting room. How did he know *that*? When I had to depart several days later, and the flowers were still thriving, Tammy came to fetch them and watch over them until they finally had to be thrown away. Presenting me with flowers became a regular ritual. I *love* flowers and I love *receiving* flowers. Never before had I been showered with such affection and attention.

And then the special "Caring Package" arrived. This, again, was before our face-to-face meeting. The package arrived at my shop one afternoon. It was a huge box; and underneath the brown paper outer wrapping was Christmas wrapping. I began opening it and kept saying to myself, "What *is* this?" There was a card on top of many small little packages. The card read:

> *My Dearest Darling Ann, I had fun putting this care (or 'caring') package together. What a wonderful thing this is—this thing called love. Without a doubt you are exciting my senses and I cannot predict what is next. Whatever it might be I will try to please you and touch your very soul. With all my deepest love, Alan.*

I opened one little package after another—each individually wrapped—each with an attached tag and a little message.

Out of the box came the following:

A Can of Sardines—*"Our first seafood dinner together."*

An Anchor Pull-cord for a Ceiling Fan—*"Hang this from the fan above your bed, reminding you I am coming home soon from a 'long cruise' and I am looking forward to shore duty with you often."*

An "S" Hook—*"The 's' hook tells you I am hooked on you!"*

Two Coffee Mugs—One tag said, *"This cup is a token of my respect for you. We will drink together."* And the other mug said, *"This is the cup I use, I will not drink from it until I am with you."*

A Small Light Bulb—*"This is the actual bulb that went off in my head when my love for you was re-ignited."*

A Recording Box from a toy that when clicked said *"Somebody loves you"*—*"I recorded this specially for you at great expense."*

A Plastic Water Bottle—*"I drank from this bottle."*

A Level—*"This level is what I will use every day to keep my love for you true."*

An Italian Coin—*"This coin is only good for one Italian lemon ice."* (He didn't know then that Italy would become so important to us!)

A MacGyver Knife—*"To fix things around the house."*

A Night Light—*"So I don't stub my toes coming to you in the dark."*

Hot Chocolate Packets—*"After the sleigh ride your mom fixed us hot chocolate. We will toast your mom."*

Hand-made Soap—*"This soap was made by my son Steve. He is into producing old-time-y products—making sausage, Canadian bacon, etc."*

A Glass Butterfly on a Stand—*"Butterflies played a role in family lore. Good omen."*

A Flashlight—*"This is a special light. This is the light to illuminate our new beginnings."*

And lastly, a Bag of Marbles—*"I finally located the marbles everyone says I have lost. I have lost my marbles, but please keep them for me in a safe place. I don't want to lose my marbles again."*

There were a few other things, but I have taken the time to enumerate what was in there because I had so much fun opening every little bit. It took me a long time to open each package and I got such a kick out of each note. I have saved each one of those little tags safely stored in a plastic bag. Boy, did he have me then! First of all, the effort he had put into the whole thing was incredible and it *did* have the desired effect on me.

Before and after that first meeting in May at Logan Airport there were more flowers and gifts. He had sent Easter flowers to Mom and to me. It was apparent that Alan was intent on making it all just perfect and he really did just that. When Alan returned to Charleston after his initial visit to the Vineyard and New England, he moved everything ahead in his mind. He was anxious for us to have our new life together start in earnest. So, again unbeknownst to me, he decided that the next time we were together we would become officially engaged. He began shopping for a ring and he booked another flight to Boston. He also shared with my sister and Eddie his intentions. My mother's birthday was on June 15th, and he wanted the celebration of my mother's 95th birthday to be the day when he would officially propose. However, he hadn't realized that Eddie can't keep a secret at all and Alan himself became too excited and impatient. So somehow the news got out and I had some inkling of what was to come. Alan had originally determined that he would let me pick out a ring and he asked his neighbor, Joe McCauley, if he would give him one of his prized cigar bands to put in a box, which he would carry to Massachusetts. Upon hearing this, his daughter-in-law, Catherine, said, "Absolutely not! When someone is opening a ring box, they don't want to see a cigar band." So Alan decided that wouldn't work too well and he shopped for a real ring instead. A few days before his departure, he went shopping. He went to five different stores and finally chose the very first ring he saw. He bought it—but he also put Joe's cigar band over the ring in the box.

Alan tells another story of his departure at the Charleston airport and what happened when he went through security. Both Alan and I have had two hip replacements and Alan has also had a knee replacement, so going through airport security is always an ordeal for both of us. For this trip Alan had the ring in his pants pocket and he left it there after he deposited keys, coins, etc., before stepping through the metal detector. He was stopped by Officer Maclean. The officer, acting very officious and Barney Fife-like, asked Alan, "Are you carrying anything you want to tell me about?" Alan knew right away what he meant, and he disclosed to Officer Maclean that he had an engagement ring in his pocket. He was asked to slowly retrieve it and show him. After a good look at it, Officer Maclean then told Alan that since he had been honest he would let it go. He was on his way (to the plane heading to Boston) with the ring still in his pocket.

I was there once again to pick him up and once again we got into the car and drove to the Vineyard. While we were on the ferry heading toward Martha's Vineyard, Alan couldn't contain his enthusiasm. He began saying things like, "I've got something in my pocket." "I've got a *ring*." And again, because I knew something was up, I could feel that excitement. He kept saying, "Do you wanna see the ring? Do you wanna see the ring?" I wasn't sure what to say. And then Alan got concerned. He thought, "Oh, dear, she is going to say no."

I, on the other hand, had felt that he hadn't yet proposed and I wasn't quite sure how to act or what to say. All was put right in our world though when we got to my house at the Vineyard, and he officially got down on his knee and asked me to marry him. And, of course, I said yes. And then he showed me the ring. And I loved it. He still felt that I would have the option of picking out something else if I wanted to. We decided that we would look at other rings and see if I did indeed want something else. He also told me about his plan to ask me at my mother's birthday, but that plan certainly was foiled because of his impatience to get on with it.

After spending another week at the Vineyard we stopped in Boston before heading on to Wilbraham and Springfield. The major purpose of that stopover was to see my daughter, Leigh, and have her meet Alan. We stayed at the Lenox Hotel and had dinner with Leigh at Brassierie Joe. We had a great time and they got on famously. It was one of the first times that I experienced Alan's interaction with waiters in restaurants and how he makes a happening out of every occasion. And Leigh could see that too. We also went shopping at Crate and Barrel so Leigh could purchase a wedding gift for a friend. We certainly didn't know then that the three of us would eventually spend many hours together, having dinner in many other restaurants—in *Italy*, no less. It was very important to me that Alan and Leigh felt comfortable with one another. He loved her instantly, which is not a hard thing to do. I discovered a Facebook exchange between them that is very sweet, I think.

A Day I will Always Remember, Dear Leigh, The day I met you I was on 'pins and needles.' I wanted our initial meeting to be special. And indeed it was. I can only speak for myself but I thoroughly enjoyed myself and felt I had made a friend. Watching you and your mother communicate was very special. You seem more like 'best of friends' than mother and daughter. May I say again, Thank You, for your gracious smiles, conversation and your company. Here's to many more such get-togethers. Very respectfully/with much love to grow in our future, Alan.

And Leigh's response to Alan:

Hi Alan, Thanks for your sweet note. I had a lovely time as well last weekend with you and my mom. And I know there will be plenty more experiences to share in the future—with less pins and needles. As I said to her, she seems very much at peace and is herself with you and I really couldn't ask for much more. And, you're right, she is my best friend. So thank you too for your company and talk to you again soon. Leigh

The next day we went to a surprise birthday gathering at an Italian restaurant, Toscano, on Charles Street in Boston for my friend, Joanne. Joanne is the wife of a former colleague of mine, Libby. Over the years I became very friendly with both of them and Libby had recently been at my house at the Vineyard when a small group of us attempted to put together a new consulting/training endeavor. That meeting had occurred shortly before Alan's second trip to the Vineyard, and I had shared with the group what was happening with Alan and I. They were delighted to hear our story and Libby determined then that he wanted us to be at Joanne's birthday party. So, of course, we showed up. We had such fun talking with Joanne's older sisters (a *very* Italian family from Boston's North End) who gave us advice that a couple should live together for at least six months before getting married. We have since been with Joanne and Libby many times and they have become special friends. Joanne is a character. She just loves our story and enjoys Alan so much. Libby is a very special person to me and, as a counseling psychologist, he is one of the people who helped me a great deal to get back on my feet emotionally after my divorce.

We then drove to Western Mass to see my family again and to officially celebrate Mom's birthday. On the way we stopped to look at engagement rings for me to determine whether I wanted something else or whether I would stick with Alan's choice. After careful consideration, I felt that Alan's choice was perfect. I wanted the one he had originally picked out.

After another nice time spent with my mother and sister and brother-in-law, Alan and I drove to Marblehead, Massachusetts to see Leigh's new apartment. David had come up from New York to spend some time in Boston and help Leigh with the move-in. It was also Leigh's birthday. Alan finally got to meet David face-to-face and the four of us shared a nice lunch and afternoon in Marblehead. We then went to the Vineyard for a few days before Alan flew back once again to Charleston. It was to be the last stretch of time that we would be apart from one another.

Alan continued with his part time work at Home Depot. But by then he decided that he would give his notice and that his tenure at Home Depot had run its course. He ordered the correct ring size for my engagement ring and it arrived in a few weeks. As my rentals started at my Vineyard house and I secured coverage at the store so that I could be away for a while, we made plans to meet up again in Florida at my Sarasota house. The plan was to have Alan drive to Sarasota from Charleston and I would fly down and meet him there.

In mid-July Alan drove to Sarasota. He arrived there a day ahead of me and started puttering at the house as soon as he got there. He loved my house at first sight. It really is quite perfect and I love it too. It is located in a wonderful little neighborhood not far from downtown, but it is a world of its own—a veritable tropical paradise. It's the perfect size too and very manageable and very comfortable, and I had a perfectly wonderful time decorating it. Alan met Tammy the night he got there, and Tammy fell in love with Alan immediately. Whenever we speak on the phone, Tammy invariably ends the conversation with, "Give my boyfriend a kiss and a hug." Tammy is the one with whom I have relied upon for anything that has to do with my house. She is a property manager and is *very* good at her job. She helped out so much when I first purchased the house and she oversaw and managed the renovation completely. To this day Tammy is there at a moment's notice when needed, particularly when we aren't around, and she will help anyone redecorate on a moments' notice! I call her the "the discount shopper extraordinaire!"

While Alan was accomplishing some fix-up chores at the house he made a trip to the Sarasota Home Depot to pick up supplies he needed and ran into an old friend who is a designer employed by Home Depot. They had worked together at the Charleston Home Depot. Alan was unaware that his former co-worker was living so close to me, believing that he was employed at another store many miles away. They were both surprised and astonished, but very delighted to meet up with one another again.

I flew into Tampa that evening and Alan was at the airport to pick me up. I remember the meeting distinctly because after a dozen or so times of flying into the Tampa airport and thinking that I knew that airport well, I somehow lost my way. I wound up coming down the escalator completely alone while Alan stood at the foot of the escalator grinning up at me. He was somewhat worried because I was not among all of the other people from my flight when they exited before me. He looked so splendid and welcoming to me as he stood there waiting. I jumped into his arms and it was my turn to feel that very lovely sense of "coming home".

We spent about a week in Sarasota just enjoying being together again and Alan got to know the area. Then we drove together to South Carolina. It was my turn to visit Alan's home—to experience his world—and to see Charleston. We stopped first at Alan's River House on the Edisto River. We stayed overnight there before arriving in Charleston. It was a nice experience for me to see someplace that had a great deal of meaning to Alan and to see the fruits of his labor. However, it would be the first and only time that I would see that house, because it was taken away from him and now belongs to his stepson.

I was, of course, excited to finally be in Charleston and to see Alan's home. The first stop was to Catherine and Steve's house to say hello to Catherine and the boys. I was finally to meet Catherine, the person who was responsible for our reuniting in the first place via Facebook. She welcomed me with warm hugs and the boys ran out to greet us and jumped into the arms of their Grandpa and their new Grandma. What fun it has been to have grandsons.

That evening we went back to their house for dinner and I was finally to meet Steve. When we hugged, he said to me "Are you crying?" And I certainly was. To me it felt like I was reuniting with my long lost son—my own son. It was an emotional experience for both of us because Steve has never really had a mother. His birth mother left him and his first stepmother abandoned him and treated him horribly. I was to be the only mother he has ever really had and that makes me very happy and proud. He called me "his new Mommy!" It has become a joke between us when I chastise him if he hasn't called us to check in and say hello. I've told him that just because he never had a mother before who insisted he keep in touch—it's *different* now!

After the short visit with Catherine and the boys that afternoon we were off to Alan's house. It is a beautiful house, but not a home—because of the trials that Alan endured during the twelve years that he lived there with his second wife. During that stay at Alan's house I was able to see and understand his world a bit more and to fully grasp the great injustice done to him as far as his home, his possessions, and his life work were concerned. And to my interior design eye the house also needed some updating and changes in décor.

The Engagement Party was scheduled for July 25th. Amy had planned a lovely gathering at their farm. I was so very happy that my South Carolina friend, Pam, decided to drive down and be there for the party. And another friend, Carey, was going to join her. Carey's son is a Charleston firefighter, so he was available too, as well as Carey's husband. It was comforting to know that a crew of my own friends would be on hand for the party. And to top it off, a very close friend of my sister's family, Odie, happened to be in Charleston at the time and he came along too.

But the very best part was that my son and daughter, David and Leigh, flew in for the party. It was only a few days before when I began orchestrating the plan and made airline reservations for them so that they could join in on the festivities. It was the very best feeling to have everyone together. We gathered at Alan's house for cocktails first and then drove to Adam's Run together. It was a great party and we had a wonderful time. Alan's best man, Ed, and his wife, Pat, were there too, and I met the rest of the family. Catherine and the boys were there, of course, but not Steve, as anticipated. Catherine made a birthday cake for Joey, Alan's eldest. It was my first introduction to red velvet cake. Catherine is an incredible baker.

Although it was so nice having everyone there, I was very aware that Steve was not a part of it and I missed him. We had to wait until the next morning for Steve to finally meet David and Leigh when the young Votta family came over to the house for a short visit. There were wonderful pictures and lots of love and laughs all around. No one would have ever guessed that things were to change so dramatically, and that the party would be only one of three occasions that Alan's family got together, because by January Alan had determined that he must sever all ties with his stepson.

The following week we left Charleston together and flew up to Hartford where I had left the Buick, my mother's old car, at Emmie and Eddie's house. Emmie and Eddie were away. We saw Mom again and then took a trip to New York: to Westchester, Long Island, and Yonkers. Alan was determined to show me around the city where I had grown up. He continued to say that I was rather sheltered as a child and there were lots of spots in Yonkers that I had no memory of. However, we did go to see our old haunts like our elementary schools, the church I attended, Gorton High School, the Untemeyer Estate, and the house on Morsemere Avenue.

We had quite an experience at my old house because as I was standing by the car across the street from the house and taking a picture of it, Alan decided to ring the doorbell. The current owner, Ed Sweeney, appeared at the front door, sandwich in hand. He welcomed us inside after Alan explained who I was. He was only the second owner since my family had lived in that house, so the Patavino name actually meant something to him. He showed us around (which was quite something being in the house where you grew up) and then escorted us out to the back where we were eager to see how it looked. My father had done considerable work on the landscaping of the entire house. There were stone stairs where the yard sloped uphill with a beautiful rock garden filled with azaleas, candytuft, and creeping pink—very spectacular when everything was in bloom. Our family was very proud of Dad's work and we enjoyed many happy family gatherings there. Amazingly, the yard still looked rather nice. Dad would have been pleased. When we were inside the house Alan noticed some NYC Fire Department memorabilia and Alan asked Ed if he knew Alexander Votta, Alan's brother, who had retired from the NYFD just before 9/11. Ed said, "Hell, yeah! We were just at an old-timers dinner last week." Another funny coincidence. Before leaving 199 Morsemere Avenue, Alan sat at the front steps and touched the step that he had touched back in 1956 when he vowed to "be back." I took a picture of that.

After the tour of our old stomping grounds we then headed back to Wilbraham and then on to the Vineyard. By this time my summer rentals were over and we could get back into the house.

We spent several weeks at the Vineyard. We worked together at the store and we worked together at the house. It was then that I officially put the store property on the market.

It was time to move forward and think about our new life together.

8

The Wedding

OUR WEDDING WAS SIMPLY a wonderful event. Everyone commented that it was the *best* wedding they had ever attended.

When we had returned to Charleston in October of 2009, we started the ball rolling with the planning of our wedding. At first we determined that we would be married at the Charleston Air Force Base Chapel and hold the reception at the Officer's Club at the base. We went there to check things out, reserved the date, and gave them a deposit. Then, on Friday, October 24th, just after we had returned to Alan's home on the cul de sac, our neighbor, Doris, came walking in the door. It was a beautiful day and the doors were wide open. Doris called out, "Yoohoo. I'm so glad that you guys are back here. I'm getting married today and I want you to come to my wedding." Now Doris was almost 80 years old at the time and she was to be married to Don, her 90-year-old boyfriend. The wedding was scheduled for three o'clock that afternoon at the church down the street, The Church of God of Prophecy. After some pleasant chitchat between us, Doris said, "Gotta run. Need to get on our wedding duds."

We had thought about that church for our wedding and had attempted to contact the pastor, but had no luck reaching him. We sat among the congregation for Doris and Don's wedding that afternoon along with the rest of the neighborhood. It was the most delightful experience. Doris is a member of a church choir and the choir was stationed on the altar of the church. As we entered they were singing such tunes as "Doris, Doris, give me your answer, do" (to the tune of "Daisy, Daisy") and other old-time favorites. We were enthralled. At the reception, which followed at Doris' house we asked about the possibility of being married at that church ourselves, and Doris gave us the correct number to contact the pastor.

Sadly, Don passed away on October 27, 2011, just three days after their second anniversary. We had just returned to Charleston after being up north and were sad to hear of his passing. At his funeral, while offering our condolences to Doris, we told her again how important their wedding was to us and that we were indebted to them for the very extraordinary experience it was for us. Doris told me to "love each other very much and make the most of every day." We were glad that they had two years together, and that they had impacted our lives.

Within a week of Doris and Don's wedding we scheduled a meeting with Bernie Levesque, the pastor of The Church of God of Prophecy, and decided that our wedding would take place at his church. We needed to stick with the date of March 13th, because it was the date that had been available at the Air Force Base and our "Save the Date" cards had already been mailed. We had not yet decided on just who would marry us and prior to our meeting with Bernie we said to one another, "Maybe if we like him well enough we will ask *him* to officiate." Two minutes after we walked in the door, said our hellos, we knew we had our guy. Prior to that we had been all over the place about making a selection. We even spoke with a priest at the Catholic Church and learned that if we wanted to marry in the church, we would both have to have our former marriages annulled, and then pay the church $5000 and wait two years. That wasn't going to work. We learned that there are priests who will perform a wedding ceremony outside of the church, but that might be expensive too because we would have to transport that official to us. It seemed perfect to us to be married right down the street from the house and then have the reception at home. The one other ingredient that was a must for us was that we desperately wanted Doris' choir to sing at our wedding. So we scrapped the original plans and moved forward with our new plans with Pastor Bernie Levesque as the man who would marry us.

Preparations for our wedding day began.

We had been in touch with several of our high school friends after we reconnected and we decided that we would ask them to attend. There were several other friends from the Vineyard, from Massachusetts, and from Florida, whom we wanted there with us as well. In all, approximately 144 invitations were sent and 108 people were in attendance—from all over the country.

My cousin, Piera, from Torino, Italy, was even trying to make it too, but it eventually became impossible for her to get there.

I had a great time planning it. I love to plan events and I was in all my glory planning this one for us. Ordering the invitations, the flowers, the cake—all of it—was such fun. It was an interesting proposition for me, considering that I was out of my element, not being from Charleston, and needing to start with a blank slate, not knowing vendors in the area. But with the help of Catherine (again) and others, it all soon fell into place.

Early on we determined that we would enlist the catering services of The Fat Hen restaurant. The owner and chef at that restaurant on Johns Island had two restaurants at the time and they had become favorites of ours. We had a meeting with talented Chef Fred Neuvill and his engaging catering manager, Amy Cook, and that was it. We were committed.

The next thing on our agenda was to contact the director of the choir of The Wayfaring Singers, and secure their services as well. Robin Rogers, the choir director, along with his wife Marianne, became the perfect persons to help us with the overall planning for the ceremony itself. My musician son, David, also helped by giving us some suggestions for the music too. Meanwhile, with the help of a business colleague of mine who had provided me the outline of his own wedding ceremony, I began writing the ceremony for our wedding. We also continued to meet with Bernie Levesque. It was at the time when Alan's serious difficulty with his stepson was in full bloom and Bernie helped Alan deal with it, giving him emotional and spiritual guidance to enable him to forge ahead and not look back. Bernie became a very important person in our lives.

I was never aware that Alan had followed me home from school that first day back in 1956, touched the steps, and made a promise that was close to his heart; he promised himself that he would return. But believe me—that story has been retold over and over and over again today. It even made our wedding ceremony and *The New York Times* announcement of our wedding. We were thrilled to have been selected to have our story appear in the Sunday Styles Section of *The New York Times*. Just two weeks before the wedding I took a chance and sent in some information about us, which customarily needs to be submitted at least six weeks prior to the wedding to be selected. We were shocked to be contacted by Vinny Malozzi, writer for The Styles Section of *The New York Times*, and we were absolutely delighted that he liked our story well enough to write about us and print it. We were interviewed and Pastor Bernie was interviewed as well, to make sure that it was all legit.

We planned a rehearsal dinner for the night before the wedding. Bernie arranged for us to use the church hall for the dinner that followed the ceremony rehearsal in the church. We sent out invitations for a "Low Country Dinner" for which we contracted with a well-known local caterer. The menu consisted of shrimp, chicken, pulled pork, corn, rice and beans. Very delicious. It had started raining when they began to set up the grills outside, but they pulled it off beautifully. And then Catherine came through once again with delicious deserts—her specialty. She made several pies and another red velvet cake. It was also my brother-in-law Eddie's birthday so we sang Happy Birthday to him and we listened to a song that Bernie introduced to the group as the song that he thought most exemplified our story—"After All" by Peter Cetera and Cher. Soon after we first met Bernie, he told us that he believed that song was meant for us. We had dinner with Bernie and his wife shortly after we celebrated our 2nd anniversary and he presented us with a framed copy of the lyrics of the song "After All" along with the CD—a wonderful gift to treasure always.

It was a special beginning to an exceptional few days in our lives. Cousins of mine flew in from California and they were able to see another cousin, who had driven up from Fort Myers, Florida. They hadn't seen one another in many years. Others flew in from all over the country. One of our friends commented, "I didn't realize that I was coming to a Broadway play!" We wanted it to be spiritual and somewhat religious in tone, but we also wanted it to be *fun*. And it was. Everyone absolutely loved it. This is the way it happened. You will see that throughout the ceremony we incorporated much of our story.

Wedding Ceremony for Ann Vincola & Alan Votta

2:45 PM   Prelude: Clarinet & Piano
3:00 PM   Medley of Songs: Wayfaring Singers
3:15 PM   Processional: "Jesu, Joy of Man's Desiring"   Bach
             Clarinet & Piano
             – Matron of Honor: Emma Migdal
             – Maid of Honor: Leigh Vincola
             – Bride: Ann Vincola accompanied by her son,
              David Vincola

Opening Words and Welcome: Pastor Bernie Levesque

Friends, we have been invited here today to share with Ann and Alan a very important moment in their lives. As most of you know, this relationship started long ago and with God's intervention their love and understanding of each other has grown and matured, and they now have decided to live their lives together as husband and wife.

The Giving in Marriage: David Vincola on behalf of his grandfather, Carmen Patavino. (With Bernie Levesque's explanation.)

Bernie: *Alan and Ann visited Ann's father's grave site at the Veteran's Cemetery in Massachusetts last May and Alan asked Carmen for permission to marry Ann. He also asked Carmen to give Ann away on the day of their marriage. The answer came in the form of a sign. The American flag in front of the stone that Memorial Day, started to flutter briskly, as Alan had experienced many days before, in a different setting, not understanding at the time about its significance. Ann and Alan have both felt Carmen's profound presence and know that he is with us today.*

Love is the eternal force that elevates life to a higher plain. It is God and it radiated from God; and if we allow it entry, it makes a significant difference in how we experience and live our lives. Love is the force that reinforces us in the good times and sustains us when we courageously face fear and uncertainty.

A miracle occurs when you find someone to love fully...and they love you equally in return. We are here today to give witness to this miracle in Ann and Alan.

Love asks that the two of you give yourselves completely to each other...to form a couple...but without losing your sense of self and identity. Ann and Alan, you are calling us here to witness your commitment to each other. You are committing to give to the other your joy, your sadness, your interest, your understanding, your knowledge...all expressions that make up life. And in this giving, you are also committing to preserve your "self"... your uniqueness, your integrity, your individuality...the part of you that has so intimately touched the other.

A book, entitled When God Winks *has had a great impact on Ann and Alan and they have become friends with its author, SQuire Rushnell. The book teaches us that coincidences are not to be ignored—that God is sending a message. In Ann and Alan's experience after many years apart, it is time for them to finish what was started in high school 50 years ago and now destiny has been served under God's divine plan.*

Alan's pursuit of Ann started when they were in the 7th grade, when Alan followed Ann home that very first day of school. Somehow he knew then that she was going to play a very big part in his life. When she was safely inside, he approached the stairs to her home and touched them and vowed that he would be back. Indeed, five years later, as seniors, they became sweethearts and one year later they went their separate ways. In October of last year, Ann and Alan went back to her old house in Yonkers, NY and Alan touched the steps again to complete the circle and the part God has chosen for them.

Declaration of Intent: Pastor Levesque asks each:

- *Do you come before this gathering of family and friends to proclaim your love and devotion for Alan?*

- *Do you promise to affirm him, respect him and care for him during times of joy and hardship?*

- *Do you commit yourself to share your feeling of happiness and sadness with him?*

- *Do you pledge to remain faithful to him?*

First Reading:

Bernie: *The first reading chosen by Ann and Alan comes from the New Testament and is Paul's address to the Corinthians about the meaning of love. While these words were composed many centuries ago, their power and truth speak to our lives today. Paul's message is that it is not what we do or accomplish that is important...it is the power of love's motivation that elevates all of what we do to a new level. I invite Edward Migdal, Ann's brother-in-law, to present these words of wisdom to us.*

Edward Migdal: A reading from Paul's letter to the Corinthians (13:1-13).

Love is patient and kind. Love is not jealous or boastful or proud or rude. Love does not demand its own way. It is not irritable, and it keeps no record of being wronged. It is never glad about justice but rejoices whenever the truth wins out. Love never gives up, never loses faith, is always hopeful, and endures through every circumstance.

Love will last forever, but prophecy and speaking in unknown languages and special knowledge will all disappear.

So, there are three things that will endure—faith, hope, and love—and the greatest of these is love.

Song:	"Ave Maria"	Schubert
	Marianne Rogers, Soloist	

Second Reading:

> Bernie: *During the time of Ann and Alan's coming together over the past year, Alan quoted the words of Kahlil Gibran and "The Prophet" to Ann many times. The words of "The Prophet" hold a special meaning to them. I invite Steve Votta, Alan's son, to present this reading to us.*

Steve Votta: A reading from "The Prophet" by Kahlil Gibran.

> *Your reason and your passion are the rudder and the sails of your seafaring soul.*

> *If either your sails or your rudder be broken, you can but toss and drift, or else be held at a standstill in mid-seas.*

> *For reason, ruling alone, is a force confining; and passion, unattended, is a flame that burns to its own destruction.*

> *There let your soul exalt your reason to the height of passion, that it may sing; and let it direct your passion with reason, that your passion may live through its own daily resurrection, and the Phoenix rise from its own ashes.*

> *And since you are a breath in God's sphere, and a leaf in God's forest, you too, should rest in reason and move in passion.*

Song: "In This Very Room"   Harris
         Wayfaring Singers

Prayers of the Faithful:

> Bernie: *Mindful of the promise that where two or three are gathered in the name of love, there love resides, I ask Anne Mateer and Adrienne Hochberg, Alan's sisters, to lead us in the prayers of the faithful.*

Ann Mateer:

- *Father, we thank you for bringing us together today to celebrate Ann and my brother's love for each other. We ask that you continue to bless, guide, and protect them in the time ahead.*

  We pray to the Lord…(People respond: Lord hear our prayer)

- *Father, we remember our family members who are with us in our minds and hearts today and who reside with you in their eternal reward. We know that the spirits of our mother and father, Anne and Alexander Votta, my husband, Bruce Mateer, and Ann's father, Carmen Patavino, are present with us today. And for Ann's mother, Helen Patavino, who wanted to share in this day too, but was unable to make the trip. You inspired them to make a difference in Ann and Alan's lives.*

  So we ask you to inspire us to express your love to those around us…especially those who are less fortunate than ourselves.

  We pray to the Lord….. (People respond: Lord hear our prayer)

Adrienne Hochberg:

- *Father, we ask that you continue to bless and guide the world…so that your spirit continues to be felt in your people….with the openness, acceptance and support that we feel here today.*

  We pray to the Lord…(People respond: Lord hear our prayer)

144

- *Finally, we invite each of us to silently ask the Lord for what we need. (Pause for a moment to allow the community to reflect on their needs)*

  Father, for these petitions held in the silence of our hearts…

  We pray to the Lord….(People respond: Lord hear our prayer)

Recitation of The Lord's Prayer:

Bernie: *Please stand and join me in reciting the Lord's Prayer.*

Song: "The Wedding Prayer"   Dunlap
         Marianne Rogers, Soloist

Vows: Ann and Alan repeat after Bernie.

I, (name), take you, (name), to be my (husband/wife), my constant friend, my faithful partner, and my love from this day forward. In the presence of God, our family and friends, I offer you my solemn vow to be your faithful partner in sickness and in health, in good times and in bad, and in joy as well as in sorrow. I promise to love you unconditionally, to support you in your goals, to honor and respect you, to laugh with you and cry with you, and to cherish you for as long as we both shall live.

Exchange of Rings:

Bernie: *From the earliest times, the circle has been a symbol of completeness, a symbol of committed love. An unbroken and never ending circle symbolizes a commitment of love that is never ending. A ring is the perfect symbol to manifest this completeness.*

Ann and Alan repeat after Bernie.

Ann: *I, Ann, give this ring to you, Alan, as a symbol of my commitment to love, honor and respect you for all the days of my life.*

Alan: *I, Alan, give this ring to you, Ann, as a symbol of my commitment to love, honor and respect you for all the days of my life.*

Wedding Blessing: "May the Lord, Mighty God, Bless and Keep You"... Tune: "Edelweiss"

Congregation, please join the Wayfaring Singers in the singing of the Wedding Blessing.

> May the Lord, mighty God, bless and keep you forever.
> Grant you peace, perfect peace, courage in every endeavor.
> Lift your eyes and see His face, and His grace forever.
> May the Lord, mighty God, bless and keep you forever.

Declaration of Marriage:

Bernie: *I ask all present to look graciously on this husband and wife, that they may love, honor, and cherish each other. And that they live together in faithfulness and in patience, in wisdom and in thoughtfulness and that their home be a haven for everything good.*

For as much as Ann and Alan have now considered this endeavor, have consented together in wedlock, have witnessed the same before this company and thereto have pledged their faith for each other and have declared the same by joining hands and by giving and receiving rings. By the power invested in me by the State of South Carolina, and as a minister called of God, I now pronounce you husband and wife.

You may now kiss the bride.

Introduction of Newlyweds:

Bernie: *My dear family and friends, it gives me great pleasure to introduce to you for the first time as husband and wife, Ann and Alan Votta.*

Recessional: "Trumpet Tune" &
            "Trumpet Voluntary"   Purcell

At the beginning of the ceremony when Alan stood at the front of the church with his best man, Ed, the choir started singing their medley of songs, including such tunes as, "Thanks for the Memories" and "The Second Time Around." This was followed by the singing of our high school alma mater, and Alan stood to encourage all of the Gortonites to stand and sing along. It was the first indication to everyone that they were in for a treat as Alan and the choir led them in song. Alan, with handkerchief in hand, continued to blubber away during the entire ceremony. He is, after all, a very emotional man and his happiness at the occasion was evident throughout. We are both apt to be brought to tears at a moment's notice and our wedding was an event that brought most of the guests to tears as well. Later at the reception my college roommate,

Ann, remarked to me that she was very taken by how Alan looked at me throughout the ceremony. She said, "I've never had anyone look at *me* quite like that!" I was very touched by that remark and it has stayed with me.

The reception that followed at the house was very special indeed, even though we had some rain clouds burst open in between which did wreak a little havoc. The food was exceptional. We knew we were getting the best and we wanted everyone to remember the food. And that they did. Alan and I didn't get to eat a thing along with everyone else, but we sure enjoyed the leftovers! The wedding cake was lovely as well. And the flowers were perfect. The music was also fantastic—from the music at the church during the ceremony to the band that played at our reception—Teddy Midnight and The Moonwalkers. My son, David, played a part in all of that, too. He selected the pieces for the processional and the recessional at the church and then he sat in on the drums later in the evening with the band as they played into the night on the deck.

The entire event from the rehearsal dinner, the church ceremony and the reception—all of it—proved to be something that people would remember for a long time.

Our hard work and planning paid off. It was an "experience," "a happening."

The following evening we were treated to dinner downtown with our old friends, George and Barbara, Gary and Ellen, and Bob and Kathy. David had already returned to New York but Leigh was still around so she joined us too. And the following day we had a lovely visit with my Vineyard friends, Barbara and Jim, and walked with them through Charlestowne Landing State Park on a beautiful day.

It was the *best* way to culminate an amazing weekend.

9

Reuniting with Others

WHILE WE REMAINED IN Alan's Charleston house that fall/winter before our wedding we started calling some old Gorton friends with thoughts of asking them to attend the wedding. We contacted our old friend Gary Bogosian and then Bob Grabowski and a few others after that. With each call we were met with instant gratification and joy. It was as if we were making a call to old friends with whom we speak regularly. After making those initial contacts we slipped into a perfect harmony of renewed beautiful friendships. And that has continued. We now even have Bob and Kathy living in Sarasota.

As we contacted these people from our high school days—people for whom we both had special feelings and with whom we shared powerful memories, and made those connections, we understood how genuine those friendships were. And the invitation list to our wedding began to grow. It was an exhilarating experience each time we made another phone call and reconnected with another individual from our past. Alan even enjoyed the pleasure of talking with two beloved and highly regarded coaches from his athletic days at Gorton. That was important for Alan because Hall of Fame coach, Larry Gericiotti, never made it to our 50th high school reunion because of illness and he passed away shortly after.

All of this reconnecting became part of our "victory tour." Everyone we came in contact with shared our happiness. It is hard to describe how much the fantastic reaction from others affected us. Whether we were sharing the story with strangers or with people who knew us way back when, we always got the same reaction—pure joy.

Just as important as reuniting with old friends became, the reconnection with Alan's family members was even more so. After many years of, frankly, being estranged from his sisters and his brother, Alan was now able to reach out to them, shedding all of the troubled past and years of not being able to be there for them. For when Alan was with Demi they never visited or saw his family at all. His family became distant. Now with his new life with me, someone who knew that family long ago, it became very important that we change that.

First we made a visit to Alan's older sister, Sis (Anne). Sis graduated from Gorton in 1958 and she married her high school boyfriend, Bruce. Unfortunately, Bruce had passed away in 2003. And, sadly, Sis' oldest daughter, Sandy, had been diagnosed with a brain tumor just about the time that Alan and I were reuniting. We made it a priority to stop in to see them in East Northport when we were in New York. That first visit was so nice, as all the others have been. Alan and I were happy to speak with Sandy on the phone one day a few months before our wedding. She had said then that if the doctor would let her, she would like to come to our wedding. That turned out to be impossible as her condition continued to worsen. We knew that it was essential to offer support to Sis in dealing with what was happening with Sandy. On one occasion after our wedding we visited with Sandy and her family too.

Unfortunately, Sandy did lose the fight and she passed away when we were in Italy in November 2010. It was very hard for us to be so far away and not be there for Sis. Sis is quite a woman and she has had to endure so much pain in these recent years. She continued to teach, but decided that 2012 would be her last year and she would retire at the end of the school year. The following February, after Sandy's passing, Sis came to visit us in Charleston. It was very pleasant to spend some quality time with her one-on-one and I believe she relaxed and felt comfortable with us. It has been very gratifying for all of us to have that closeness back.

Then there is Alan's younger sister, Adrienne, or Teenie. Although they are a year apart in age Alan and Teenie were in the same grade at Gorton and thus, Teenie was a member of the class of '61 too. Teenie and I were good friends at school. We were in a "Y" group together. Incredibly, I was able to locate a photograph of that group taken at a photographer's studio in 1960. Amazingly, Teenie and I are standing as a pair together. Teenie attended the Fashion Institute in New

York and there she met and married Arthur. Growing up, Alan and Teenie had been very close, so much so that within the family Teenie was called Alan's shadow. But once again he had lost that closeness which, frankly, became a missing link in his life. So when we were in Sarasota in January and early February before our wedding, I felt that it was important that we get together with Teenie and Artie and make that reunion happen.

Teenie and Artie had been wintering in Jupiter, FL for several years and they had agreed to drive over to the west coast to Sarasota to visit us. It was a great experience for all of us. It was the first time that Alan and Teenie and Artie had the opportunity to spend time together after quite a few years. And, of course, it was special for me to be able to see Teenie again, meet Arthur, and know that we were bringing this family together again. As he exited their car upon their arrival in our driveway, Arthur said to me, "I have a sister-in-law! I like that." We have since shared many happy hours with Teenie and Artie as they made Charleston a stopover each time they traveled back and forth to Florida.

We haven't yet gotten together with Alan's brother, Sonny, but we have talked on the phone many times and that is also something new for Alan. Alan is very pleased that he has been able to let Sonny know how much he means to him. Sonny's daughter, Susie, and her husband, Keith, came to our wedding as the representatives of that family. Susie has also hosted a Votta Family Reunion at their home during the past several summers. Catherine and Steve attended the reunion in 2009 and we tried to get there the summer of 2011, but we just had too much going on to get there. We hope very much to be at the next one.

There have now been cards and notes and letters back and forth among all of the Vottas, with a lot of sharing going on. Alan sent copies of the letters he had written to his daughter and his stepson to Sis and Teenie. I encouraged Alan to do that. I felt it would help if they could offer their perspective on the situation and provide support, which of course, they have done. They have agreed that Peter has behaved despicably (especially when they read his very harsh words in his response to Alan), and they have boosted Alan's morale throughout. Being able to bring his siblings back into his life has also brought another dimension to Alan's existence—a dimension that did not exist before. It certainly didn't happen during his previous marriage. He had been a stranger to his own family.

And along the way we have reconnected with so many other folks too. My cousins have been in the mix, as well as friends of both of ours who provided us with enduring friendships over the years. We find ourselves very often expounding on the pluses and advantages of Facebook, because Facebook has, in fact, been instrumental in making many of those reconnections happen. And beside our very intriguing Facebook story, there is another story that should be retold here too.

Alan had a famous cousin. That cousin, who was very close to him growing up, was Brian Piccolo, the Chicago Bears football player and the subject of the movie, *Brian's Song*. Brian died in 1971 at the age of twenty-six. As teenagers Brian and his brothers, Joe and Don, lived in Fort Lauderdale, Florida, and they played football. Alan spent several summers in Fort

Lauderdale with the Piccolos and he, too, played football with Brian. The cousins also had fond memories of being together in Yonkers, New York, when the family gathered at their grandmother's house. I have since heard lots of stories about the goings on of those frisky boys. (See photo from 1957).

As was the case with the rest of Alan's family he had lost touch with both Joe Piccolo, the eldest brother, and Don Piccolo, the middle brother, as well as Brian Piccolo, the baby of the family, before he passed away. When we started spending time in Sarasota together Alan mentioned that he knew that his cousin Joe lived somewhere on the Gulf Coast but didn't realize how close it was to Sarasota. It was Clearwater—just 45 minutes north of Sarasota. Alan contacted Joe and an instant reunion on the phone occurred—each speaking of love and happiness at reconnecting. At that time Alan also learned that Joe's mother, Alan's Aunt Irene, was in a nursing home in Clearwater and was approaching her 101st birthday. We visited Joe and his wife, had a lovely lunch with them and then visited Aunt Irene on her birthday. It was quite an experience for Alan. His Aunt Irene, his mother's sister, was the last of nine siblings. Although Aunt Irene was not really able to communicate, Alan was able to touch her and whisper in her ear and feel a closeness to his own mother that was long gone.

Following that encounter with Joe, Alan asked about his other cousin, Don, the middle brother. Although Alan was close with Brian, he was equally close to Don. Alan learned that Don had just moved from Baltimore, Maryland, to San Diego, California and was living with another cousin of theirs and helping her out at her home. Alan called Don. What a wonderful conversation they had. Another reunion. They lovingly talked about the past and couldn't understand why they had lost touch. And they promised to *stay* in touch from that moment on. Before hanging up Alan threw out a comment to Don. "Don, whatever happened to Judy Tork?" Judy had been Don's girlfriend when they were fifteen years old in Fort Lauderdale. Alan had no idea why that name had come to him, but he blurted it out. Don responded, "Gee, Alan, I haven't thought of her or heard that name in over 50 years." But it got Don thinking because he really *had* thought about Judy over the years and often wondered about her. After they said their goodbyes, Don went on Facebook to look up Judy. There were about six Judy Torks listed, but the very first was *his* Judy Tork. He was certain of it. And he contacted her right away.

When Alan phoned Don a second time, Alan began the conversation by saying, "This is Judy Tork's attorney and she is suing you for a paternity suit." Don's response: "Really? I never even touched her."

As this story then unfolded—Don learned that Judy was single and living in Myrtle Beach, South Carolina, ironically about an hour and a half north of us in Charleston. And with Don being single as well, they started a nice phone and email relationship similar to what we experienced. That took place in October 2010. (At this point we were kind of sad that we had reconnected with the Piccolos *after* our wedding because it would have been really nice to have them there to celebrate with us.) We were aware that Judy and Don were communicating, but we were unaware of how far their relationship had gone until we received a message from Don while we were in

Italy during the month of November. He said, "Alan, I am so friggin' happy that you mentioned Judy's name to me!" He also informed us that he would be spending a week in Myrtle Beach in December and we would have to get together. What did *that* mean? We could only speculate that things had moved on to another level with them.

After we returned from Italy and Don had arrived at Myrtle Beach, we made plans to meet at a restaurant in Charleston. We were the first to arrive and then in walked Don, Judy and Judy's daughter and two granddaughters. There were hugs and kisses all around and more hugs and kisses. What a time we had. And what a reunion it was. On the one hand it was just fabulous that Alan and Don, the cousins, were together again after all these years and it was *very* apparent that the relationship between Don and Judy was more than just friends. We remained at that restaurant for over seven hours. We had arrived at one o'clock and we didn't leave until almost 8 pm. The restaurant management and wait staff catered to our every need and they allowed us to have this special reunion. They enjoyed the entire event themselves.

Fast forward. By February of 2011 Don moved from San Diego to Myrtle Beach and is living with Judy in her condo. We have spent several pleasant afternoons with them and we talk regularly. And they have visited with us in Sarasota. Judy is a wonderful person and I have loved having both of them in my life as well. They are very happy together. Another success story for Facebook! So whenever I hear of anyone being hesitant to join Facebook, it perplexes me. I feel that the benefits of Facebook far outweigh any drawbacks.

Aunt Irene, the mother of Joe, Don and Brian Piccolo, died in April of 2011. We were still in Sarasota and we made the trip over to Fort Lauderdale for her funeral. Teenie and Artie also attended. On that occasion we met Brian Piccolo's wife, Joy, and his three daughters. Although Alan knew Joy and had seen the girls when they were very young and Brian was still alive, he certainly had had no connection with them now. It was very nice to make that acquaintance again. And this whole experience of reconnecting with all the Piccolos has made Alan realize just how much his cousin Brian had meant to him. He is determined to keep his memory alive, as so many people who never knew him at all, still do. Interestingly, Aunt Irene lived forty-one years after Brian's death and Brian's jersey was number 41.

During the ten years that I had been spending winter months in Sarasota I had been very happy to reconnect with my cousin Carl and his wife Rita. Carl's mother, my Aunt Ginny, was one of my mother's younger sisters and the only one left of her five siblings. The Sousas had moved to Florida many years ago. My parents had visited with them at times when they spent winters in Florida, but I hadn't really seen them at all. And I didn't know Carl's four children either. So with my time in Florida I was able to begin seeing them regularly and I have enjoyed their family immensely, even joining them on holidays. I've grown to love his wonderful growing clan and especially his five grandchildren. On both my mother's and my sister's trips to Sarasota, we drove to Fort Myers to visit with all the Sousas prior to my aunt and uncle's passing. That was a good thing.

The first time that Alan and I got together with Carl and Rita was an event itself. I don't know whether Carl and Alan knew each other back when we were in high school, but the four of us had so much fun together; it was like we had rekindled an old friendship. Another example of coming together.

Whether it has been reconnecting with loved ones—former boyfriends and girlfriends, sisters, brothers, aunts, uncles, and cousins or old schoolmates—the process is a wonderful, exhilarating experience that has added another dimension to our lives.

PART THREE

Our Future

10

Moving On

WE CERTAINLY FEEL THAT every day since March 21, 2009 has been beautiful. We give thanks every day for the blessings we have received. We consider ourselves extremely lucky and feel that nothing can interfere with our happiness. That said, it is important to acknowledge that in other areas, the path has not always been that easy: we have had to deal with some difficult situations along the way and those issues have taken up considerable time. We've been confronted with concerns over our combined financial picture, and with legal issues particularly the complex situation with Alan's stepson.

Although we are so blessed to be living the life we have now, we somehow meet each day with a little trepidation in anticipation of when the next shoe might drop, or the next wrinkle will present itself. We certainly hope that we will be able to look forward to a comfortable retirement and continue to do the things we want to and live a secure and simple life. We have learned that just having one another is enough and we do not need to be at all extravagant.

But at the beginning of our time together we were saddled with the responsibility of maintaining three households—or money pits. And the bills continued to mount. We were confronted with selling property and ridding ourselves of "stuff" that had become burdensome, and in an unfavorable housing market, that was going to be difficult at best.

I had, over the previous years, been fortunate enough to rent both the Vineyard house and the Sarasota house from time to time, which miraculously enabled us to keep going and provided some additional income. But it has been a lot of work. We are forever having to put out fires at one or another of the houses and it hasn't been the easiest thing to keep it all together. When we tell people that we are living in three such lovely locations, it sounds idyllic. But we are the first to admit that it isn't as ideal as it appears. No, it has been difficult. I constantly find myself stopping us in our tracks and forcing us to take the time to enjoy ourselves and take advantage of the beautiful places we are lucky enough to inhabit. But we have been confronted with problems nevertheless: such as a new hot water heater at the Vineyard (summer of 2010); other plumbing problems at the Vineyard (summer of 2011) which cost thousands; a stolen air conditioner condenser in Sarasota while we were in Italy (November 2010); a burglary also at Tahiti Park, Sarasota (November 2011); other repairs and maintenance issues in Charleston. None of it has been fun and it has caused angst and money. And, of course, we have had to be constantly on the move, going from one location to the other. But through it all we carry on and look forward to the day when we can be released from some of it and can get to an easier place for two 70 year olds. This is the time of life when we should be enjoying ourselves every day and not have to deal with such problems on a daily basis. We know that we can get there.

On top of it all there have been hundreds and hundreds of hours consumed with strategy sessions in dealing with the dilemma with Alan's stepson. It started with the many letters to him to build a case for Alan by simply appealing to Peter's sense of right and wrong. Alan was fully aware that the probate on his deceased wife's will was over and that he had opted to sign off on it rather than go to court. But he felt in his heart that his stepson would surely see that Alan's life's work could not be wiped out and that he, Peter, should not benefit from it all. Alan never expected that his so-called loving stepson would turn on him and not understand. But that is what has happened. His stepson has been so harsh and so hard-hearted and has refused to see the situation from any vantage point other than his utter greed. It troubled Alan so much in the beginning that he lost much sleep over it all and needed to seek counseling to help him through. We spent many hours talking about it, which resulted in Alan drafting letters to his stepson. The letters essentially became a therapy of sorts for Alan. It gave him a chance to pen his feelings and to fully understand his own perspective about what had happened.

The letter writing and laying out his position was the start, which in turn, led to Alan's decision to cut off all relations with Peter and his wife. That happened before our wedding so they were not in attendance and they were no longer invited to take part in our lives at all. It wasn't until after our wedding, as we searched for an attorney to handle the case, that Will Swope entered the picture. Will is the son of Alice Swope, a dear old friend of Alan's whom he worked with when he was in real estate. Alan has maintained a close relationship with them over many years. When Will heard from his mother what was going on in Alan's life, he said to his mom, "I want to represent Alan. He's family."

Then began many hours of communication and meetings with Will to first establish the case against his stepson and to move it along. We worked with Will for over two years with numerous court hearings, affidavits, arguments, and complaints, taking up lots of time. We were forever drafting questions and positions to get to the next step. All of that resulted in the necessity of selling Alan's Charleston house. The house finally sold in March 2012 and we left Charleston for Sarasota, now our permanent residence. Moving out of the Charleston house and ridding ourselves of the numerous bad memories inherent therein was a very positive step.

Alan had been resolved to move forward no matter what the outcome. Ultimately, Alan felt that the struggle had been worth the effort merely to attempt to show his stepson the wrong Alan had been subjected to. Whether Peter will ever see that, acknowledge it, or accept it in his own heart is another matter.

That leaves us with the ultimate decision of trying to sell most of what we own in real estate so that we can truly move on and make our dream of living in Italy become a reality. The Vineyard house has been on the market two different times now, with no takers. The bursting of the real estate bubble has been a real problem for us. Everyone knows it is not the best time to sell anything and that is the problem with which we have been confronted. I was extremely lucky to find a buyer for the store property on the Vineyard at the right price. However, that transaction was fraught with difficulty too. Before closing on that property, an oil leak was discovered which resulted in numerous hours and thousands and thousands of dollars in a clean up, all of which rested on my shoulders. So instead of being ahead of the game after that sale, I found myself behind the eight ball once again. On top of that, the Sarasota house is "under water." On that score we are confronted with the decision of sticking with it, and hoping that the market improves, or just walking away at some point. Time will tell on that one. And, hopefully, the real estate market will improve soon.

Throughout all of this we have continued to work very hard. We have cleaned out and shed tons of baggage in terms of "things." We have held yard sales and taken box loads of articles and furniture to consignment shops and have sold many items. That has actually been a very positive purging. We have much too much stuff. We know we need to pare down. And, in essence, it has all made it easier to think about moving out of any one of our houses when the time comes. We are *ready*.

So that brings us to an explanation of just what our dreams are and what we would like our future to be.

11

Italy

*I*TALY AND OUR Italian heritage have come to play a major part in our lives, giving us an antidote to the more negative aspects, opening up new vistas, and providing us with another monumental and exciting milestone. Because of our Italian heritage and direct line from our grandfathers, we have become Italian citizens!

I had been to Italy several times over the years, but Alan had never travelled there. In fact, one of his first thoughts after his wife passed away and he was free to do what he wanted was to take a trip to Italy and visit the town of his grandfather's birth, Venafro. He had applied for his first passport and was thinking about taking that trip just before we reunited. In our initial discussions and emails, we talked about Italy and the hometowns of our grandparents. We discovered that Alan's grandfather and my grandparents were both from the Molize region and had left the towns of Venafro and Montelongo, respectively (a forty minute drive apart—a mind-boggling thought considering the size of the country—destiny!), to emigrate to America in the early 1900s. We jokingly have said that it is probably a good thing that we didn't marry and have children together when we were young because we may be related! When Alan's grandfather left Venafro, he went first to Glasgow, Scotland, and married Mary Gillespie before bringing his new wife to Yonkers. My grandparents, on the other hand, went to Mount Vernon, New York and that is where my parents were born.

Alan and I began talking a great deal about Italy and knew from the beginning of our new relationship that we would be traveling there as soon as we could.

We started reading about Italy and Alan was introduced to several books about living in Italy to set the stage for what we/ he might expect. I had already been convinced that I wanted to spend some extended time in the country of my ancestors, but I needed to have Alan understand that as well. We also began to communicate more with my Italian cousin Piera who lives in Torino, Italy. Alan had the opportunity to speak with Piera on the phone several times and he soon learned what fun she is. She is an amazing individual and I couldn't wait until Alan met her. At the same time my daughter, Leigh, began to seriously consider what it would take to live and work in Italy: something she had discussed with my father before he passed away, and after she and I had taken a trip together to Italy in 2002.

Leigh had been to Italy several times—the first time with me when she was 13 years old. (When our children were young my first husband and I usually did things a little out of the norm. Special trips became a sort of "rite of passage" for our non-Jewish children who found all of their friends having bar mitzvahs and bat mitzvahs. His father took David to Africa and I took Leigh to Italy. In retrospect, I guess Italy was a good idea for Leigh and it had a major impact on her. Little did I know that then, though). She went to Italy a few times on her own as work-related trips. The story I have included in the Afterword section of this book shows how the visit we made together to the town where my grandmother was born laid the foundation for our dream of living in Italy. Leigh is the real writer in the family and I am very proud of her accomplishments. She wrote the Montelongo story after our trip taken in March of 2002. She never published it thinking that it "wasn't her best work;" but I have continued to share it with many people because I think it is so good. I have her permission to share it here. I feel it tells a lot about our family, our interest in Italy, her love for her grandfather, and about the very special bond she and I have with one another.

That trip to Italy with Leigh in 2002 was my fifth trip to that country. My first experience in Italy was in 1967 when I met my mother's relatives in Torino. I was able to bring greetings from my grandfather to his sister whom he hadn't seen in fifty years. It was a very moving experience for all of us. My parents had also taken two trips to Italy during the '80s and had visited those relatives as well as other relatives of my mother's in Naples. Cousin Piera came to the U.S., and my sister and nephews met all of them on different occasions in Italy. Leigh has spent considerable time with Piera in Italy as well. We consider Piera a very important part of our very close extended family.

In preparation for an extended time in Italy on a WOOF program (Willing Workers on Organic Farms), Leigh decided to try to find out more about where her grandfather's forbears derived from. We didn't know much about that history and Leigh started digging around. By searching on the Internet she found Marco Micone (Micone was my grandmother's maiden name) who was originally from Montelongo, Italy, the town we knew to be where my grandmother was born. Marco lives in Canada and is a playwright and translator. Leigh contacted him and they determined that we indeed are related. He invited Leigh to stay at the family homestead, which he still maintained in Montelongo. At the same time, I was planning a trip to England for an antique shopping spree. I became intrigued with it all and decided to meet Leigh in Italy and accompany her to Montelongo. Leigh's story in the Afterword will give you the rest of the details of that trip.

Sharing all of this with Alan made the desire to go to his grandfather's birthplace even stronger for him, and that's when he began reading books about Italy and consuming all he could get his hands on about the Italian way of life. Leigh had been living in Marblehead, Massachusetts, and was working in public relations in the food and restaurant industry. But she was seriously thinking about taking the huge leap of leaving the U.S. and living in Italy for a time. She knew she needed to give it a go. She had been studying Italian for a few years; taking courses as well as individual lessons with an Italian tutor. She also started researching the process of applying for dual citizenship and she connected with Peter Farina of ItalyMondo, a company in the business of helping Americans secure their Italian passports and dual citizenship. The three of us then decided to contract with Peter and really get the ball rolling to become official citizens of Italia.

After Alan and I connected with the process too (a process that became much more involved as time wore on), we made the decision to take a trip ourselves—our honeymoon. Leigh was ready in November and so were we. We flew together to Rome and we lived in an apartment together in Termoli, Italy, where we established residency, a necessary step to expedite the dual citizenship process. While we were living in Termoli we were able to visit Montelongo too, so Alan got to meet the people we had come to know there and he understood how important Montelongo had become to Leigh and I. Then we visited Venafro, the town where Alan's grandfather was born and saw the house where Giuseppe Votta lived.

Leigh had then planned to take up residence in Florence and we spent some time there too. We spent a little more than a month in Italy and terminated the trip in Milan so that we could spend some time with Piera in Torino. We were also able to see Piera's brother, Tony, and mother, Yolanda, too. Sadly, both of them passed away the following summer. We left Leigh living in Florence where she remained until she secured employment in the south of Italy, Puglia, the heel of the boot. This is ironic because, although she expected to make a life for herself in Florence, she wound up back in the south, the area where we started our trip. Leigh then began working for a company called Southern Visions Travel as a marketing consultant. In the spring of 2011, the SV team opened La Cucina at Gelso Bianco, a villa and cooking school, which, of course, fit in with Leigh's culinary background. Leigh then moved from Monopoli to Ostuni. It was all very exciting. It is the region of Italy to which we would ultimately like to move, because we loved it so when we spent only a few days there on our first trip. Just prior to our second visit, Leigh was contacted by House Hunters International, and they filmed an episode about her and her life in Ostuni, which ultimately aired on HGTV in the states. Embarking on a new venture, i.e. Leigh Vincola, Lifestyle Coaching and Personal Cartography, she now spends part of the year in the states and part in Italy conducting retreats for her clients.

We love the south of Italy, particularly the region of Puglia. While we were in Italy the first time, we visited a few towns in Puglia, but didn't spend as much time there as we would have liked. Then when Leigh lived and worked in Ostuni and the surrounding area of the south, and we were able to more fully appreciate life in Puglia, we became convinced that spending part of our lives there, too, would be our ultimate desire. If we are able to sell real estate in the U.S., we feel that we could then either rent or buy property in Italy. We have thoughts of perhaps doing a home exchange at first and spending about six months in Puglia to determine if we would really like it. I have been trying to learn Italian and have finally become serious about the challenge. I have taken a few courses and I am using Rosetta Stone. I realize how difficult it is to learn another language at this age, but I am approaching it with new vigor. Alan, on the other hand, has no patience for it. He believes that when he gets to Italy and immerses himself in life there he will learn eventually. You should see him conversing with Italians in his made-up Italiano. It is pure Alan. Somehow they know what he is saying all the time with his abundant gestures and many hugs and kisses.

What we both do know, however, is that the Italian way of life is totally compatible with our way of thinking. We love the style, the slower pace of life, and the FOOD! We believe that we can be happy there and that we can meld into Italian life. And, of course, with my daughter spending time there as well, it makes it all the more compelling.

Our papers finally came through and we officially became Italian citizens. After a trip to Miami to the Italian Consulate, we then had our Italian passports in hand. We embarked on our second trip to Italy in July of 2012. We stayed with Leigh in her Ostuni apartment and had an absolutely fabulous time reaffirming our desire to spend more time there. We have also taken advantage of Alan's military benefits and have utilized the Space-A Program (Space Available) to fly to Italy at no cost. That has surely made it all the more accessible to us.

Both of our trips were incredible experiences. We loved every second. We drove over 3600 kilometers through the regions we visited on the first trip and felt very at home wherever we were. Since we had rented an apartment, we lived as Italians and not as tourists. I still would like Alan to see other parts of Italy and see some of the major sights of the country, but he doesn't feel so inclined. He feels very comfortable with what he has already experienced and we both essentially feel at home in the region of our ancestors. We love our heritage and we are certain that our parents and grandparents appreciate that it has become an important aspect of our life together.

The opportunity to wax more eloquently about Italy and our relationship to it will be the subject of another book.

12

High School Reunions and Planning a 50th Reunion

*I*T IS IMPORTANT to note how reunions play a part in our story. We would be celebrating our 50th high school reunion in October 2011 and we actually were somewhat responsible for the whole thing coming together in the first place. We served on the planning committee with our friends Gary Bogosian, George Ampagoomian and a few others. George and Gary and their wives attended our wedding. George was the president of our class, Alan was vice president and Gary was treasurer.

Alan and I did see one another before our coming together in 2009. That was in 1986 at our 25th Gorton High School Reunion. It was held at The Rock House in Hastings, New York. Ironically, that is the place where Alan's father played many times when he had his band. And it also was the place that two years later (in 1988) our family celebrated my Mom and Dad's 50th wedding anniversary.

I attended that reunion with my husband, Keith, along with another couple.

I really don't remember much from that reunion. It was well attended and I was happy to be there, and it seems (from pictures I have now seen) that everyone had a wonderful time. It was probably the *only* time that my husband ever consented to join me at a function like that during our marriage, since he had no personal interest in it at all. Consequently, like in most other social situations in which we found ourselves, I wasn't able to be myself nor to act and feel and say what I wanted. Instead, I sat by his side all night and, as usual, became concerned about what he thought, how he acted, and whether he was having a good time. I know that I didn't speak to that many people—just a few.

I don't remember even laying eyes on Alan until we were almost ready to leave. I have to say that it didn't affect me at all to see him or say hello to him. But, boy does he remember how *he* felt! He said that he was looking my way all night and he felt that my husband was staring at *him* all night. And what he specifically remembers is that when we said hello and gave each other a hug, he whispered in my ear, "Thanks for the memories." He had rehearsed that line and had decided that was what he was going to say to me. I remember only that he had whispered something, but I was unsure of just what he said. It didn't have much affect on me. I had no idea of his feelings at that point and how I still figured in his life. Alan was married at the time to his second wife, but she did not attend the reunion with him. I don't remember seeing Alan's sister, Teenie, either, although she had a hand in helping to plan the reunion.

After the dinner, Alan tells me that he went to Gary's house and continued to talk about seeing me and to bring up my name to the group that had gathered there, no matter what the topic of conversation.

Reunions are funny things. The 25th reunion was the first planned by our class. When you are 43 years old, one is fairly well established in life, with a career most likely at its peak. And if you feel good about yourself and content with whom you are, you'll feel comfortable attending a class reunion. I certainly felt that way. I thought that I was happily married, had two great kids, and had just embarked on my consulting career that eventually led to some very productive and successful years for me. I do think that when you attend a reunion like that, you wish to advertise to the world that you are doing okay. As the years move on you realize some of that stuff is really not important at all! At the time Alan had already retired from the Navy and had begun his new life with a new wife and a new business, but he also realized that life wasn't exactly what he had wished it to be. The handwriting was on the wall even then.

Jump ahead then twenty-five years to our 50th high school reunion and how things changed. It has been so special for us to reflect on what our high school days meant to us, and that is why we are so grateful to be able to spend quality time with those very same people today. They are very important to us.

Our 50th reunion was to be held at the Marriott Hotel in Tarrytown, New York, the weekend of October 15, 2011. Planning the reunion turned out to be loads of fun. The committee shared many laughs together, and we each played a significant role and worked hard to make it an extremely successful event. We scheduled a monthly SKYPE call and took on individual tasks. Beside the schedule of events and getting it all up on a website, the most important task was to locate and contact classmates and encourage attendance. We left no stone unturned and we were able to locate approximately 80% of our graduating class. We soon realized that the number of deceased classmates had grown considerably since our last reunion—up from eight to twenty-five within the ten years from the 40th reunion in 2001.

The schedule of events for the reunion started with an informal cocktail gathering on the Friday night with about forty-five classmates in attendance. We even had some individuals from other classes attend as well. On Saturday, a group of us drove to Yonkers and met in the school library at Gorton. The current principal of the school met us there, along with a few student guides who took us on a tour of the building. That was an experience for us. The building has certainly seen better days and it is in dire need of a major overhaul. But it was quite incredible to walk the halls again, reminisce about our days there, and generally feel in awe of where we were. We all remembered how we circled the halls every morning way back when, walking hand-in-hand with our current squeeze. It was a *must* that one would arrive well ahead of the first bell in order to do that.

A home football game was rescheduled by retired Coach John Volpe, a favorite from our era, and so respected in retirement that the powers-that-be quickly made the change so that we could enjoy the game on our own field. Gorton won the game against Lincoln High School 38-0. They did us proud. It seemed very strange indeed to walk out of the school and hear our names announced over the loudspeaker (Class of '61 President, George Ampagoomian, Vice President, Alan Votta, Treasurer, Gary Bogosian, Homecoming Queen, Sharon Nolan, and Lady-in-Waiting, Ann Patavino) and then meander around the field and sit in the bleachers that we had sat in so long ago. And when I looked out at Alan standing next to Frank Forcelli on the sidelines, watching the game, it was kind of a sweet but eerie feeling, knowing that they had so many fond memories of playing football on that field themselves.

The main event of the reunion was the banquet on Saturday night. After the committee set up the room with decorations, we changed into our fancy duds and met for the cocktail hour prior to the dinner. It is very hard to describe the electricity in the air that night. Smiles and hugs and belly laughs and more smiles and hugs and belly laughs. Before heading into the banquet room we posed for a class photo. There were 117 people in attendance that night and 73 classmates from the class of '61. We congratulated ourselves on those numbers. At the banquet we even had three of our former teachers join us. One of our planning goals had been to see if any teachers from our era were still alive and well enough to be part of this event. Originally five teachers were to attend, but two had to cancel because of illness. They ranged in age from 78 to 91.

But the biggest congratulations to us as a class and to the committee, is that we were able to raise $7500 as a donation to YPIE, Yonkers Partners in Education. From the very beginning of our planning, we determined that we wanted to try to give something back. There was much discussion on that until we settled on YPIE. Because Gorton is such a different place now than when we were students, the current student population has few resources with which to develop careers and go on to higher education. That is where YPIE comes in. The organization offers on-site counseling to students to help them set goals and move on to college or trade schools. Our gift was warmly received. We accomplished that by holding a silent auction and holding a raffle. I was in charge of the fundraising and it was very gratifying that it all worked out so well.

The event culminated at a brunch on Sunday morning at the home of Helene and Ken Orce in Scarsdale, New York. What a way to end a spectacular weekend. And what a beautiful home. The comments and feedback from classmates were over the top. Everyone expressed how well everything turned out—Friday night, Saturday, Saturday night, and Sunday. Every minute of it was unbelievable.

For Alan and I, the reunion was even more special I think than for anyone else. We had left the Vineyard on Wednesday, the 12th of October, visited my mother first and then drove on to New Paltz, New York, to stay with Gary and Ellen at their house. I had been in charge of ordering the gifts and mementos for the reunion and those items had all been delivered to Gary's house, so I hadn't yet seen what I had ordered. Staying at Gary and Ellen's beforehand enhanced the whole experience for Alan and me. It gave us the opportunity to spend some quality time with them and to really set the stage for what we would experience with everyone else. Together we unpacked everything, filled tote bags, and then organized and loaded it all into our cars for transport to the hotel. Gary was the perfect logistics person for the entire event. He was so organized. What a great guy.

And certainly the fact that Alan and I were now a married couple attending our 50th reunion together made it a unique happening. It was quite interesting to hear that some people were under the impression that we had been together all along: then there were others who didn't even know that we were a couple in high school. But *everyone* was delighted for us and they couldn't be happier that we were now married. Alan, in his inimitable way, even made a point of thanking the crowd for attending our personal reunion and anniversary!

As I talked about attending a high school 25th reunion and what it meant to all of us at that age and time of our lives, I soon understood that seeing those same friends, after another twenty-five years had passed, was another thing altogether. At 68, one looks at everything mighty differently I believe. One doesn't need to prove anything any more and you've either made it or you haven't. You are comfortable in your own skin by then, or you aren't, and one's outlook for the future, hopefully, is genuinely positive. Or so it certainly seemed to be the case for those of us who gathered for this our 50th reunion.

What does attending a 50th high school reunion mean? It means that we have made it this far and that we wish to look back and think about where it all started. It means that we are content enough and happy enough with our lot in life to want to reach out to those people whom we knew then, and left behind when we were eighteen years old. It means that we are happy for the people with whom we were able to connect and see that they have been successful and are still loving life. It means that we are sad about those we have lost and we can remember them with fondness. And it means that we planned well for a very memorable occasion. It also means that we still have energy and still are enjoying life. In fact, the hotel staff was totally amazed at how we had the stamina to dance with such vigor well into the night. As we departed at the end of the weekend, the question on everyone's lips was, "When will we get together again? Do we have to wait another ten years?"

The committee held a follow-up meeting via SKYPE and made the decision to plan to hold another reunion in 2014 at the same location.

To me all of this reconfirms the idea that to look back is a positive thing, and that reconnecting and reuniting makes life a great deal more interesting and meaningful.

13

Life is Good

W E START EACH DAY by turning to one another in bed and saying "I love you." And Alan always adds, "For a very long time." And at the end of each day, Alan says to me, "I had another wonderful day."

Alan says things like "I love being me again. I love being in my own skin. I've learned how to live life again." He approaches every day in a positive way. When we were on one of our trips up and down the east coast, he said to me, "I can look out and see a beautiful world that I appreciate with renewed vigor. I see life so totally differently now."

Time had to pass for Alan to realize how he was forced to live and how difficult his life had been. It has taken many hours of talking and understanding from me, family, and friends for him to realize how horrible life was with both "The Baby Maker" and "The Evil One," the terms he has now begun to use to label his first two wives. At the same time, we have come to realize that we both lived in rather abusive relationships—mostly verbally abusive, where power and control issues made for uncomfortable living. And we both found ourselves powerless to make change. When you are in a situation like that you often ask yourself, "Is this normal? Is this the way others live?" And you never quite know the answer to that. Alan and I discuss those ideas a lot now. We can see that it is very hard to get out from under the control of another when you are consistently made to believe that it is your fault and that if you tried harder it might get better. I know for me, when I was going through my divorce, it took a good friend to influence me enough to realize that what I experienced wasn't normal and that I deserved better. It wasn't until I read lots of books about being in an abusive relationship that I understood exactly what I had experienced in my marriage. I learned that when an individual experiences verbal abuse in his/her own life, they only know how to replicate it; that is, they use power over those closest to them to make them feel strong and purposeful themselves. That is exactly what I experienced. And now I have been able to share that insight with Alan and help him understand how his life was affected by a struggle against power. It is interesting that when we were packing to move out of his house, I came across a newspaper clipping that Alan had apparently saved quite a while ago. It was a Letter to the Editor entitled "Emotional Abuse." He may not have outwardly acknowledged he was emotionally abused, but the mere fact that he saved the article says it all. And it certainly spoke to me too. It read as follows:

"Insidious" is the perfect adjective to describe emotional abuse by spouses or partners. It is the sucker punch of a bad relationship. You never see it coming, but it causes grave damage, both to the victim and to children who may witness this behavior and grow up thinking it is normal. Unfortunately, many times nobody outside the immediate family recognizes this form of psychological battery; abusers typically display this behavior only in the presence of their victims. Thus, if and when victims finally gather the wherewithal to get out of these relationships, they appear to acquaintances and certain relatives to be abandoning their families. The abuser also is deceitfully crafty. These emotional predators use their dysfunctional attributes to convince their victims that: *They are always wrong in a disagreement; *Something must be mentally wrong with them; *They will never amount to anything resembling success; *They have nothing worth contributing to a discussion; *They cannot do anything right. They have an uncanny ability to control the relationship to the point that anything the victim says or does is portrayed in a negative light.

Clearly we both lived all of that. But that was the past. Today things are so different with a loving partner. When you are on a natural high everything is good: everything looks good; you feel good. All is right in the world and you are at peace with the earth. When you are living under a cloud everything is so-so and you don't see the beauty around you or what is special. That is what has changed for both of us.

Alan has told me numerous times that the second my name popped up on his screen that first day and the moment we embraced at Logan Airport, he knew. He knew that this time we were going to be married. As a matter of fact, as Alan looks back, he realizes now that 199 Morsemere Avenue, Yonkers, New York became his "Mecca." He has also shared with me now that he often dreamt about me and I would pop into his mind every time he went through a rough period. Very often the mere thought of me would help get him through the negativity that engulfed his life. In his mind, it was unfinished business. He felt that one day we might be back together.

Our coming together has also brought more spirituality to our lives. I don't think we will ever become "religious" per se, but we do feel a greater degree of God in our lives. And Alan has continued to see visions of departed loved ones. He revealed to me one day that our very dear friend, Billy Johnson, appeared to him standing before him with his famous grin on his face. We are certain that Billy is very happy that we are together. Billy was a special friend to both of us and we are so sorry he isn't here to share our new found joy.

Another vision that appeared to Alan—and absolutely stunned him—was his vision of his Uncle Frankie. Uncle Frankie was Alan's mother's little brother who died when he was seven or eight years old in a freak accident when a truck backed up, tires hit the curb, and the tailgate flipped open and hit him on the top of his head. He died instantly. The significance of this is that when Alan was about four years old he was critically ill with pneumonia. During the worst of it his doctor made a house call (doctors regularly did that then) and gave Alan an injection of penicillin, a new miracle drug that was top secret and used only on Allied soldiers to date. Alan was one of the first children to be administered this new drug and no one was sure it would work because of the stage of his illness. That night while his mother was attending to him and fearing the worst, Uncle Frankie appeared to her. He smiled at her and told her that Alan would be all right—that it wasn't his time. She looked back to Alan and his eyes opened and he seemed to have come through the crisis. The drug worked. The story was an important one for the entire family. And the fact that this had all come back to Alan's attention gave him emotional pause. His new life has given him the ability to reflect on these powerful images of the past. {As I sit here writing these words and reciting them to my husband, he is weeping softly. After five minutes of emotional breakdown and hugging and kissing, he is saying to me, "Penicillin in Italian is 'Patavino'. None of this would have been possible without you entering my life."}

In addition to those visions, Alan had another powerful experience. As we put our respective houses on the market we succumbed to the lore of burying a statue of Saint Joseph to aid in the sale of the house. When we bought the statues at a religious store we were told that the prayer to Saint Joseph would play an integral part for a successful sale. Alan became committed to the prayer and he began to pray and talk to Saint Joseph on a daily basis. One day he was stunned again when he clearly felt Saint Joseph's presence, giving him a peaceful overall feeling, and a sense of calm that the houses would sell—eventually. We really don't know what to make of all of this, but we like to think that it means that we are supported by these spirits and the bleachers in heaven continue to fill up on our behalf.

There were two other items in that "caring package" that Alan had sent me before we got together the first time. Those items inevitably became very significant to me. One was a small coin that had engraved on one side of it, "A friend loves at all times." And, on the other side, "Friendship is the golden thread that ties our hearts together." Alan's tag attached to that coin was, "My best friend." And that is what he calls me—as well as his wife, his lover, his buddy, his shrink, etc. But *friend* is the most meaningful of all. The other item in the package was a memorial card from Alan's father's funeral. The front side of it was a copy of one of Alexander Votta's paintings. It is a house on a country road with lovely trees. It is beautiful. On the reverse side it reads:

In Loving Memory of
Alexander G. Votta
May 11, 1917–June 12, 2007
Our Dad

Honesty, integrity, and loyalty, Our Dad had those traits. He was a researcher, a teacher, a person of resource. Our Dad was an "educator." He encouraged, supported and guided us. He wanted us to want to learn. Our Dad was a nurturing person. His values were clear to all. Our Dad, the artist, musician and writer. Our Dad was talented. He was a storyteller, a jokester and a humorist. He loved to laugh. Our Dad always had time for his children, his grandchildren. Our Dad was special because he was Ours. He was, Our Dad, Our Grandpa, and Our GG. We will miss you. Love, Your Family

That card was an important little piece of the puzzle for me since I hadn't known Alan's father all that well and I needed a better look into their family. What I realized then is just what a remarkable man Alan's father was. He was truly a Renaissance Man. He was talented and accomplished. We have three of his paintings hanging in our home now and that is very important to me. And, when I hear Alan's sisters speak of how very much like his father Alan is, I am reminded once again of how lucky I am to be with this incredible man. He may not possess all of the talents and gifts of his father, but he is blessed with his own gifts and talents that make him a truly remarkable individual and my husband.

Alan's sister, Teenie, after reading a draft of this book had these words to add, and I think they are important to quote here:

As an aside, I've been regarding Alan as a reincarnation of the good traits of my parents. He has the beautiful, gentle, kind, nurturing, brilliant mind of my mother and the golden hands, inquisitive mind and personality of my father. My parents shared many wonderful traits for that matter; both loved all people regardless of station in life, religion, race, etc. Both were very talented. My mother did the NY Times *Sunday Crossword puzzle every week; she was the best cook on earth; and she knitted beautiful sweaters for us. Most of all, they listened to us. Our weekend breakfasts were a time when we all sat around the table and discussed life, politics, science, religion and an entire plethora of things. Each of us, regardless of our age was able to speak our mind and give our opinion on any given subject. We were raised in a democracy. We thought the world worked that way.*

That gave me even more insight into the Votta family and the traits that Alan inherited. When we were young we spent so much time with my family and Alan was fully aware of what my family meant to me, but I needed to know more about what made Alan the man he is. This certainly helped.

Another very important ingredient to the life we now share is laughter. Alan and I find ourselves laughing all the time. We laugh and laugh and laugh. So much so that I have gotten to the point of having to yell "STOP" before I have an accident and pee all over myself. The first time Alan started spouting his completely made-up Italian, I really couldn't control myself and I *did* have an accident. He never ceases to amaze me with his quick mind and even quicker wit. Alan thinks I am quite humorous too. I never thought of myself in that way, but he gets many chuckles from my "being me"—a "me" that I never knew existed. It has taken our renewed love to bring this out. Sometimes I find myself looking into his eyes, as we stand holding one another with my arms around his neck, feeling a weird sense of déjà vu. I look at him and I can see the eighteen year old that I loved back in 1961. He can move his head in a certain way or say something or turn his eyes toward me and I remember exactly the same gesture or expression from so long ago.

We also feel that we are making up for lost time in the bedroom! Sometimes we feel like we are still eighteen and can be mighty frisky—and we don't need any help with little blue pills or such. Our friends tease us as they recognize the fact that it is sometimes hard to get us out of bed in the morning—we seem to sleep late a lot! One encounter stands out in our minds on this topic. After we had become engaged and we were still on the Vineyard, we were departing the parking lot of my store when we met the FedEx lady. Alan had sent flowers to me once again and we had intercepted the delivery. We stopped her and chatted a bit as she handed over the box of flowers. Of course, Alan had to relay the story of our getting together. She was enthralled. But her only comment was, "The sex must be great!" We were stunned, but we looked at one another and with wide grins on our faces, we said to her, "Yes, it certainly is."

We have learned so much *about* one another and *from* one another. We all grow and change a great deal as we progress down this path called life. Our experiences mold us, but somehow, we may be lucky enough to hold on to some of the qualities that made us who we were as young people—when we were carefree and without the responsibilities of adult life. Somehow we find ourselves integrating the past with the present on a daily basis. That's why it was so special for me to hear about everything that Alan remembered—the fun times we had at school with our friends, as well as the fun times we had with my family. It has been an important ingredient in our new life together.

Thus the concept of reuniting and attending reunions became integral to the telling of our story. The whole idea of reconnecting with old friends has been extremely important to us and we are convinced that it is one of the things that has enriched our lives. Alan has made a point of telling each and every friend and family member just how much they mean to us and how much they are loved. And at our now frequent get-togethers Alan is usually on center stage making everyone laugh uproariously—especially after a few glasses of wine!

I have spent many hours editing this manuscript and reading it back to Alan. Invariably, I become aware of him staring at me with tears in his eyes as he listens carefully. And sometimes we both stop and have a good cry again about what we have experienced. They are tears of joy and we are grateful for what we have.

So this is our story. It's a love story and a fairytale rolled into one. We hope you will think so too and that you will seek to find lost love and reunite with those who meant something to you long ago.

Afterword

Montelongo

By Leigh Vincola

MY GRANDFATHER'S NAME was Carmen Anthony Patavino. He was born in the Bronx in 1911. He was the youngest of four. His older brothers, Pasqualle and Giovani, were born in Italy, and he and his sister Lucia were born in the U.S. His parents, Anna Maria Micone and Michele Patavino left the village of Montelongo in 1906 for New York. After Carmen's birth Michele planned to return the family to Italy, disenchanted with America, but he fell ill and died. The widowed Anna Maria raised the four children in the Italian neighborhood of the Bronx. Carmen's brothers, significantly older than he, worked for an auto mechanic, and at the age of fourteen he joined them. Years later Carmen fell in love with the company secretary, Helen Marano, and married her. Together they had two daughters, five grandchildren, and celebrated their sixty-fourth anniversary.

Everything Carmen did he did with care and he did it well. He told long stories with precise detail and patience, while his long slender fingers made silent gestures in the air. His skin was thick and dark but not coarse. He had hands that everyone loved to hold. In his ninth decade he had a full head of hair, mostly white, with still a few streaks of black. On his left wrist he wore a watch he bought at Bloomingdale's in 1962. He died wearing that watch. He was small but strong, insisting on using his body, until the very moment it was no longer possible. His house was neatly appointed with relics of his long golfing career, German beer steins collected during the war, Frank Sinatra and Dean Martin records, newspaper clippings about the New York Yankees, and framed photographs of his beloved family. Every well-used tool in his garage had its own place next to his meticulously neat and maintained Buick. Year after year he grew brilliant azaleas and roses in his backyard. Carmen was a man who understood that his body and mind could take him where he wanted to go. Step by careful step he created a life worth admiring. He took great pride in the things he loved. He kept his family strong. Carmen lived ninety-two years.

I had planned a five month solo trip to Italy. I wanted first and foremost to spend a significant amount of time out of the country, knowing that soon my busy schedule would make even a short trip impossible. I chose Italy because it was a way for me to experience something new, and at the same time remain physically and emotionally close to my family and connected to home. My goals for Italy were to visit with a beloved Marano cousin in Torino, to discover the village of Montelongo, see the

sights, learn the language, and fall in love with the lifestyle. I was
to fly into Milan where my cousin would meet me, but beyond
that my itinerary was quite loose. I was confident in letting my
mood and circumstance fill in the holes of my time abroad.

As my departure date grew nearer I spread an old map of
Italy out on the dining room table. With a pink marker I circled
the places that I thought I'd like to go. Torino, La Cinque Terra,
Napoli. My fingers traced the mountain towns of the Abruzzi,
but did not land on one named Montelongo. I was only able
to circle the general area where I thought the village must be.
It remained something of a mystery but I never doubted that
I would get there. I imagined that I would arrive there by bus
alone, and I would spend the day wandering in silence trying
to imagine people who were my own, living out their lives one
hundred years ago. I would attempt to connect and give profound
meaning to a place that gave me only a blurred conception of
my roots. I imagined that I would approach and converse with
strangers, in a language that I hardly spoke, hoping that the
names Micone or Patavino would sound familiar. I imagined I
would take photographs and leave at the end of the day feeling
like I had done something important. I did not, in anyway,
imagine what I was to actually find. For one week before I was
to leave on my visit, Montelongo took on a much larger significance. With the help of the Internet I not only located the
village, but I located a man, who I now know to be my mom's
second cousin, named Marco Micone from Montelongo. Marco
and I quickly exchanged e-mails, phone calls, and photographs
of our families. My mom and I pored over each picture for any
resemblance that would make us certain of family. It was in the

eyes. We learned that Marco and his family had left Montelongo for Montreal when he was a teenager. He has lived there ever since, marrying and raising two sons. Recently retired, he spent his career teaching Italian and writing plays, in French, about Italian immigration to Canada. Marco was gracious and kind, openly welcoming us into his life, as if he had been waiting for us to find him. During his childhood Marco had been very close to his grandfather and remembered him saying that he had a sister who had gone to America. He hadn't heard of her since.

"That would make us second cousins," Marco said to my mother over the phone.

"Yes, I guess it would, and our fathers, first cousins."

"I still own my grandfather's home in Montelongo. It is pretty empty right now, but you are welcome to stay there as long as you wish. Let me know when you will arrive and I will ring my Aunt Lorenza. She has the key. She lives in the house next to the fountain."

Within a week we had become family, and thus there was no other way to experience Montelongo than from the house of our family's origin, the house that our relatives had once called home. My mother decided to accompany me to the village and suddenly my trip to Italy had a distinct focus.

Grandpa was happiest when we were all together gathered around a dinner table or scattered among chairs, couches, laps, and pieces of the floor. He was proud of what he and Grandma had created. But this pride and happiness didn't begin with us. It had a past as well. A man of such strong family values was not just born into the world. Those values came from somewhere. It now seemed possible to put the pieces together and observe the place where they were formed, not only for myself, but more and more each day I felt I needed to do this for Grandpa. I longed to touch a piece of the past from which he had become estranged, and contemplate a history that had been somewhat forgotten by the rest of us.

There were no stories of the Patavinos like there were from Grandma's family, and for so long her family was our only connection to the old country. We had filled in the Marano family tree and had been exchanging letters in broken Italian and English for years. With his brothers so much older than he, his father dying young, and his mother so burdened with everyday survival, Grandpa had lived much of his life without an immediate connection to his roots. There was something that told me that nearing the end of his life, he wanted to reconnect, that he wanted to be reminded of, and encouraged to contemplate, his past. He never told me any of this. I just knew.

With the passing of Grandpa's 90th birthday and the engagement of his first grandson it seemed as if the generations would soon be shifting. Grandpa was a fighter and was in no way ready to leave us; he wouldn't be until he no longer had the energy to put on his white gardening gloves and putter in his backyard. This day would not come for two years, but with the discovery of Marco it seemed clear that now was the time to go. Working around my mother's schedule, we planned a mid-March visit to the village, and Montelongo became my trip's sole purpose. Everything else became periphery. Five days in a small village would connect my past and present in ways that I never imagined.

On the secondary highway that travels south along the Adriatic coast, the towns anticipate summer. Pastel homes and hotels are boarded up, empty, or under construction. With them comes a loneliness that cannot be escaped. The surf rolls in against concrete jetties in shades of bluish brown. A silver Fiat pulls into a petrol station where the north/south road meet, a road running east to west. Inside the car my mother and I pull out a well-creased map of Italy and lay it on the consol between us. We locate our destination, the Village of Montelongo, the township of Campobasso, the region of Molise.

"What do you think? Should we keep going?" my mother asks.

"Probably about another hour, right?"

"That would be my best guess."

"I don't know. What do you think? It'll be getting dark by the time we get there. We could stay in one of these creepy hotels or just take our chances and go."

"You sure they know we're coming?"

"Marco said he would call them. Let's go. I don't want to stay here."

On we drive as the waning March sun sinks lower in the uncharted sky in front of us. At this moment my mother and I enter into a world completely of our own and are safely guided through, a time and place that will highlight our lives as mother and daughter. Winding our way through early spring hills of wheat there is nothing left to do but follow the blue and white signs that lead to the village. The soft hills rise and fall around us in shades of the freshest green, its few inches of growth remaining motionless in the breeze. Nervous excitement runs through us as we giggle, shedding our roles of mother and daughter and letting them slip down the hillside and back into the hotel room in Umbria where we began that morning.

The road leads us past a cluster of stone houses where it intersects another. Outside the houses, the sidewalk is lined with potted geraniums and rosemary bushes. We continue on.

"I think that was it," I say.

"Yeah, me too. I saw a fountain."

Already heading out of town and down the other side of the hilltop, I stop the car and turn around, bringing us back to Montelongo. A group of older men standing in the town center had watched us carefully as we passed, knowing that we would be back momentarily. You don't just drive through Montelongo. It's on the way to nowhere.

We parked the car and I checked my back pocket for the name of the woman, scratched on a piece of notebook paper, who supposedly held the key to Marco's house. I turned to my mom, and took a deep breath. We were in the heart of old world Italy and I was about to leave the comfort of our rented Fiat and become, as never before in this country, very American. My mom stayed in the car leaving me to be our representative while she watched through the rear view mirror. In my jeans and New Balance sneakers, I walked slowly across the cobblestone toward five older men wearing wool caps. Their complexions were bathed in the warm glow of evening, each face a true reflection of Mediterranean twilight. They discontinued their daily chatter to watch me approach.

"Bona sera," I say.

"Sera," one of them responds.

"Dove una donna che se chiama Lorenza…?"

I referred to the piece of paper in my pocket, feeling foreign and young. Simultaneously all five men pointed their equally short arms to a small old woman, standing behind a glass door, watching as we tried to make sense of her village. She knew exactly who we were and that we were looking for her: but she waited there and watched as the events unfolded and solidified in my memory, until my mom and I knocked upon her door.

We were greeted by Lorenza, her sister Pepenella, and Pepenella's son, Pepino. These first moments were a cluster of confusing introductions, however, clarified by warm hugs, two cheeked kisses, and the presentation of food and drink. Lorenza was a slight and wiry woman who wore large glasses and short hair. I watched as she stuffed a used tissue under the sleeve of her sweater and I thought of my grandmothers who had often done the same. Time after time I would learn that traditions I assumed belonged to my family actually belonged to this country, to a whole nation of people. Pepino, short for Guiseppino, is Marco's cousin on his mother's side, the side not related to us. But what I've learned growing up in an Italian family, is that the word cousin can be used to strengthen almost any relation. I have ten first cousins. But there are at least thirty others whom I refer to as my cousins, with no need to explain whether they are actually my second cousin once removed, from the other side of the family, someone I actually have no blood relation to, or a first cousin of a close family friend. It doesn't matter. Family is family. And cousins make it better.

Lorenza's house, where the three of them lived together, was small and had the simple yet refined feel that distinguishes an Italian home. In the front room, there was nothing more than a knotted wood dining table, five short backed chairs, and an old television set back in the corner. The room was dimly lit. Behind it was the kitchen where an open fireplace glowed with slow burning olive wood. Two child-sized wooden chairs sat on either side of the fireplace. The wall above the mantle was dotted with copper plates and color prints of Jesus. From the ceiling hung fresh sausages from animals raised, butchered and processed in this very village. This house would be our base camp for food and direction for the next five days. My mom and I sat in the front room and replenished our travel-weary bodies with pastries, and our first Montelongan café.

Pepenella was a round and toothless woman, dressed all in black. She did not look much different from the many other widowed women we would see tending and preserving their home of Montelongo. She wanted to speak to us, tell us of her pained leg muscles, of the clams she would cook for dinner, and of her love for her youngest son who had returned to the village to care for her. She wanted to tell us of her life because, unlike the rest of the town, we didn't know anything about it. She spoke with a thick Molisian accent, dropping the end of each word, leaving a sound, low and breathy, to fill the room.

Pepino, equally rotund as his mother, stood in front of us and reached to the left of the door, under the window, where a rack full of keys hung. He asked his aunt which keys belonged to Marco's house. It was then I realized the role this woman and this house played in Montelongo. Lorenza was the key holder. She held them for all the families who no longer live in the village, and they first came to her when they returned. The keys hung there motionless, waiting to be touched, while their owners buzzed about in large cities, living lives vastly different from the ones they once knew. But eventually they would return, if only for a short visit and be reminded of what they left behind. Lorenza held the heart of a village once vibrant under her front window.

Pepino left us to relax and settle into Marco's house. He offered us the most important staple items he could at the moment, espresso, and an unlabeled jar of hand pressed olive oil. "Tomorrow we will buy provisions," he said. We thanked him and went silent.

My mom and I shuffled around from room to room for what seemed to be a long time. The house was small, only three rooms, but the act of tracing the steps of our grand-mother and great-grandmother made it seem huge. The front room was the largest and least furnished. Its musty walls were painted white and an old leather couch sat unwelcom-ing against the far wall. I looked inside a large armoire and found children's blankets and beach towels which seemed, at the moment, completely out of place. In the kitchen was a fireplace that I imagined had not been lit in a long while. Above it hung a poster advertising a production of one of Marco's plays. A simple table with a plastic checkered tablecloth sat in the middle of the room with four chairs around it. Next to the sink stood an espresso maker and four small wine tumblers. The bedroom was off of the kitchen separated by a door with a fogged glass window. In the room were two single beds made into a double, one dresser, and two night tables. "It is not the Hilton," Marco had said to us in his beautifully blended French and Italian accent. The house was sparse and damp, as a summer house often is in winter. Marco and his family come only once a year in August when many other Montelongo townspeople return from Montreal. It is then that Montelongo breathes with life that it hasn't since the early part of the last century when families sailed across the Atlantic in search of something more. Most of the year the village whispers a quiet song of desertion. Old stories travel from widow to widow through the black threads of the clothing worn day after day.

With dampness seeping into our bones, fatigue setting in, and two hours to kill before dinner; we wanted to change into more comfortable clothes. I lent my mom my long underwear and we made the double bed and got in it. We laughed and sighed in disbelief. It was March of 2002, but we could have been anywhere in time. Warming up under quilts, my mom and I played hang man and tick-tack-toe until the moon rose over Montelongo.

We walked arm in arm across the stone studded streets that had narrowed in the darkness. We clutched each other closely, fending off the unexpected cold known to this craggy hilltop village. The sound of our own footsteps broke the silence. A woman stood with a broom in a yellow-lit doorway and watched us with questioning eyes as we walked past. By tomorrow the whole village would know who we were, but tonight we remained on the outside. I wanted to tell her, "I am Marco Micone's cousin; my great-grandmother and great uncles were born here; this is my mother." But I didn't. I squeezed my mom's arm tighter, thankful for her company, and continued into the darkness.

Cimitero

On the outside of Montelongo lay the village cemetery. My mother, Pepino and I approached slowly on the dirt road in Pepino's 1960's Fiat. The air was significantly warmer, making an effort towards spring, but the northern wind of winter still swept down the greening hillsides rattling the just blossom-ing olive trees. The air blew through me and I found myself detached, as if watching from somewhere else, as my mother and I stepped into the past. There sat tombs, stacked four high, above the ground, each displaying a black and white photo of its occupant, the year of their birth and death, and at least one brightly colored plastic flower. In Southern Italy the soil is too rocky, and there is no money to dig. My eyes scanned the first row; Nicolina Carlone, Stefano Brunetti, Lucia Macciagodena, and there were their eyes, staring back at me. Born mostly around the turn of the century, these men and women of Montelongo represented the generation that stayed behind. Five or six names made up the majority of the gravestones, one being Micone. Michel Micone nato 1878 morto 1973, Rocco Micone nato 1900 morto 1997, Rosina Micone, and so on. All related, somehow, to me. I thought how glad Grandpa would be to know that his bloodline is long lived. At ninety he expected at least a few more good years, and he got them.

We slept in, letting the sun rise high enough to spill in through the balcony and warm the kitchen. It rose with a strength that we had not felt since arriving in Montelongo. I lingered in its luxury while my mom rinsed her underwear and then her hair in the kitchen sink. In my pajamas I made her a cup of tea, milk and one Equal, or the Italian version thereof, and sat at the kitchen table to eat buttered biscuits. While her tea cooled I waited for my mom to join me. Pepino had planned an afternoon outing to Termoli, the closest large town on the Adriatic coast where we would find a woman known by everyone as Zia Maria. She was the oldest living person from Montelongo and perhaps she would recall my great-grandparents. Pepino left us to our own morning which sunk slowly and deeply into us both.

My mom and I stepped outside to the balcony leaving the sliding glass door open behind us. The cloud-speckled sky was still. Nothing, not even time, seemed to separate this century from the ones that came before. In the distance lay the next village, Santa Croce, perched atop the neighboring hillside. It is visible from here, but from inside the walls of Montelongo, it is not even a thought. It is like another world, separated if only by a slight contour in the land. Its people are separate from the people of Montelongo; they have their own fountain, their own key holder, their own stories. In the distance smoke hovered over a pile of burning olive wood. It smelt sweet as it traveled down into the valley that separates the villages. I gazed over layers of red tiled roofs. Their clay was cracked and flaked giving way to time and weather, but never completely giving up. Was it standing here on this balcony one hundred years ago, looking out over the same scene, that my great-grandparents decided to leave?

"Do you feel like you've been here before?" I asked my mom.

She laughs a little and says, "No, this is like nowhere I've ever been before. Do you?"

"I don't know."

I wanted to say yes, to say that somehow it is strangely familiar, that I knew that this place has been a part of me before, that I have stood on this balcony and looked out on these fresh hills, but I confessed no, somewhat disappointed in the ancestral connection that had not materialized in my subconscious.

"Did your grandma ever talk about this place?"

"No, not that I remember really. No one ever did. As soon as they left, they cut all ties in order to start over. And, none of them could read or write, so there was no way to communicate with the ones that stayed. It was the future they talked about, not the past."

"Yeah, I guess that's true.... How do you think they got to Napoli from here?"

"I don't know, it already seems so far away."

As I stood there I contemplated the bravery of shoving off with small children to an unknown place. They had probably never been to Campobasso, let alone Napoli, let alone New York City.

My mom hung her underwear on the banister and shook her cleansed hair towards the sky. She was managing quite well with the limited comforts this house has to offer and I felt proud of her self-sufficiency. We unfolded the yellow plastic lawn chair collapsed in the corner and brought out two chairs from the kitchen. I settled into one chair with my legs stretched out on the other and opened up the green notebook that held our notes. Our attempts at making a family tree had become a confusing mess of Pepino's handwriting. It seemed every woman was named Rosina or Lucia, and every man Michele, Guiseppe, or Pasqualle. I did my best at untangling the web of relation until, in my mind, the pieces we had made sense. My mom was fully reclined with her eyes closed next to me. She dozed in and out of sleep and I watched her breathe and thought how lucky I was that this sixty-year-old woman sat beside me. Our concerns right then were not influenced by our individual lives, they were exactly the same. For the purposes of the newly detailed family tree this woman who sat next to me is by title and definition my mother. But in solidifying this relationship on paper, we were opening up others in reality. My mother was becoming the friend and travel companion that she had never been before. I too closed my eyes and indulged in the warmth of our quiet balcony.

It was only hunger and the sound of two solitary church bells that drew us back inside. My mom and I began to pull out, one by one, the makings of lunch, and placed them on the table: a crispy loaf of bread, a bottle of olive oil, an assortment of prosciutto and salami, fresh parmesan and mozzarella cheese, and roasted red peppers. These we would tug and drizzle and spread and cut until we had created our own, perfectly constructed panini. For dessert, oranges and apples, cut and peeled, sectioned and shared with care.

Sitting across from my mom, our spread of food between us, we tiptoed back to her childhood, to New York, to the stories whose details I'd never heard. She told me of her Sunday afternoon visits around the neighborhood when she would join her grandmother and sit on folding chairs under grape arbors in Mt. Vernon. She told me of the bed on which her grandmother would lay sheets of freshly cut pasta. She told me of warm summer nights when three generations would gather on one stoop. She told me that outside of these homes she sometimes found ridicule rather than pride in being Italian-American. She told me about when there was nothing, there was always enough for that special something and that made all the difference. A handmade dress for Easter Sunday, or a new doll at Christmas left my mother and her sister with a sense of gratitude for the smallest gifts and pleasures. I imagined my grandpa as a young father home from the war, scraping by with next to nothing, spending his days at the auto body shop and evenings with his wife, daughters, and garden. He took great care of the things that he loved. He nurtured them with patience, persistence, structure, and strength. As the stories spilled from my mom's mouth across the table, Grandpa's words swarmed my head. "Whatever you do, do it well, and enjoy yourself doing it," he had said to me once over the phone as I aimlessly wandered through young adulthood. It may seem like a piece of simple and straight forward advice for a grandfather to give his granddaughter, but time after time those words have made me stop and think, and most importantly slow down, and attempt to fully carry out with success whatever I was engaged in. This is the best advice I have ever received and sitting there with my mom it became clear that Grandpa lived a happy life by following the advice himself. He was becoming my hero.

Peacefully filled we let our bodies process the food and words they had absorbed. As the rest of Montelongo shut its windows and bedroom doors, so did we.

Zia Maria

We approached Termoli at about mid-afternoon. Pepino, who had ridden in the back seat of our rental, continued his chatter interrupting his own stories to direct me towards the home of Zia Maria. We rang the bell and a slight shuffle could be heard from three flights above. The shuffle grew louder until a pair of wrinkled ankles slipped into a pair of shaggy green slippers appeared on the landing above us.

"Zia Maria," Pepino called out.

"Ciao Guiseppino," a stuttering but strong voice answered back.

We climbed the stairs to meet her, but already Zia Maria had welcomed us into her life.

"Oh Madonna. Estati Uniti," she repeated throwing her long fingers towards the sky.

"Il cugini Americani, Madonna mia," she continued as we exchanged kisses and followed her up the stairs.

We entered a comfortably furnished living room, much more contemporary than those we had become used to. Here we were given more kisses from Zia Maria's son, and his wife Rosina. We sat down and Rosina brought out a tray of Campari and Perugia chocolates. Pepino made introductions around the room. Rosina turned quickly to my mom and me and said "sorelli?" They were surprised as many others had been and would be, to learn that we were in fact mother and daughter, not sisters. We had been told before how much we look alike but never had anyone questioned that a generation separated my mother and me.

"Zia Maria, these women have come to find out about their ancestor Maria Micone, born in Montelongo. Do you remember anything about her?" Pepino asked. The ninety-five-year-old Zia Maria paused and thought intently for a moment, repeating "Maria Micone" to herself. I showed her the family tree I had drawn in hopes it would help jog her memory. She repeated aloud every name written on the paper in a monotone voice gasping for what seemed could be her last breath between each name.

"Rocco Micone, Lucia Micone, Guiseppi Micone, Regina Micone," she said until she reached my great-grandmother's name. She paused once again and finally belted out, "Si, Maria Micone!" as she threw her hands up in what seemed like surrender rather than recognition. There was no emotion in her voice that affirmed our search. But it didn't matter, Zia Maria was certain, no matter who we were and what our story was, that we were related not only to Maria Micone, but somehow to her. It seemed as if anyone could have walked in off the street and she would have had the same reaction calling them il cugini Americani. For a moment her arbitrary insistence tumbled my confidence towards doubt. I looked around and thought to myself, "What are we doing here?" We have come all this way to drink Campari with strangers searching for a connection that was lost a century ago. I looked at my mom and I knew she was thinking the same thoughts. Sitting next to me on the couch she whispered in my ear, "What the hell are we doing here?" and we both smiled, unable to control a small outburst of laughter that had been flowing unconsciously for days. Her voice was not full of dread or disappointment, but rather of a light and youthful acknowledgment of what is.

And then Rosina turned to me and said, "Si, lo vedo negli occhi." I see it in the eyes.

Zia Maria had no distinguishing memory, no revealing photographs, but the trip to Termoli was worth the effort. We thanked them for a pleasant afternoon and Zia Maria got up to walk us out. Again she descended the three flights of stairs shaking her hands towards the heavens on each landing. She walked us to the street where the car was parked, prayed to the Madonna one last time, and turned around to climb the stairs and finish her Campari.

As we waited for our homemade pizza dinner, Lorenza and Pepenella offered my mom and me seats in front of the fireplace. I sat down in the small wooden seat which barely held my rear and felt the dry warmth of the flames. Pepenella passed with confidence and ease between the living room and kitchen. A widowed mother needs hardly to speak in her own home. It has become her life's companion. She clings to it with tenacity and rarely leaves it alone. On the television the nightly show has begun. Posto nel Sole, an Italian nighttime drama filled with love affairs, scandal, and manipulation. These two toothless women watch from their hilltop village with anticipation and desire. They will live out the remainder of their lives like this while unknown worlds, on television or otherwise, play out in truth and in fiction around them. Sharing dinner while watching a silly sitcom on TV, my mom and I have often thought of Lorenza and Pepenella, who are no doubt exactly where we left them. I wonder if like us, it is not the actual drama that they are captivated by, but rather the feeling of reacting to something together.

After dinner and coffee and Pepenella's refusal to let us help clean up, Pepino offered to take us to the bar for a gelato. In Montelongo there is one business and that is the bar. It does not have a name, just a sign that reads BAR on the outside, facing a lonely street. There was a soft murmur coming from inside. A man behind the counter talked quietly with his friend who sat under dim lights alone, drinking espresso and smoking cigarettes. The cigarette smoke swirled under the light and inside the air felt heavy and stale. Pepino greeted and introduced them to his two female American companions. They took little interest in Pepino's animation as he encouraged us to make the very best ice cream selection. My mom, who never eats chocolate because it gives her a headache, ordered a chocolate cone. When she does eat chocolate it means she is happy, for that happiness is enough to fend off any discomfort. I am not surprised that on that night she feared not the onset of pain. Right then, it could not touch us. We strolled back outside leaving the scene inside the bar to continue without our interruption. The three of us, gelatos in hand, walked without speaking to the middle of the street, the center of Montelongo. We heard footsteps from behind the church and a solitary voice called out to the darkness. The only other sound was our own. Pepino pointed to a few houses and told us, as he had all week, that in them, there is nobody, that their owners have moved away.

Municipio

Pepino walked us to a building that sat nondescript behind two homes on the west side of town. On the outside was a sign which read Municipio, meaning for our purposes, Town Hall. Inside we found Antonio De Michele. He sat reading a newspaper in a folding chair with his feet crossed on his desk. Pepino explained once again that we were searching for any information that would confirm our connection to Montelongo and our relation to Marco. Having to spend the day out of town, Pepino assured us that Antonio would help us with whatever we needed. With the green notebook clutched under my arm we moved into the records room where a long table separated a bookshelf full of records from the rest of the room. My mom and I stood on one side of the table, Antonio on the other. Behind it hung a blue and red flag which proudly proclaimed the town where we had found ourselves. Feeling a little foolish I snapped a photo. Next to that hung a Xeroxed sign that read "Non Fumare," Do Not Smoke. Antonio stood in front of it, pulled a cigarette towards his mouth and lit it. This, I regret not capturing on film.

We started with what we knew for certain: the names and dates of birth of my great uncles, Pasquale and Giovanni, my mom's uncle Patty, and Uncle John. From the shelves behind the table, Antonio pulled out a large leather bound book which documented all births in Montelongo dating back to the 1700's. Puffing on his cigarette Antonio opened the book and let the pages fall and separate slowly from one another one by one. He showed no fear as the burning ember at the end of his cigarette dangled above his town's highly flammable history. I thought this funny, but was not surprised, for this was Italy, where rules and laws are only a suggestion, meant in most circumstances to be broken. Under Micone their names were there, scrolled in thick almost illegible cursive across the wide page. Pasquale and Giovanni, born to Maria and Michele. Except there had been another. The first born, Pasquale, two years prior to my great uncle who as it seemed was named after his deceased older brother. He had lived only one week. Grandpa never knew he had another brother, or my mother, another Uncle Patty.

We then moved to the marriage files which were held together in a similar leather bound book which sat impressively large in front of us on the table. My mom did not know the date of her grandparents' marriage, and neither did my grandpa. I thought how strange that once they are gone that information is so easily forgotten. I know that my grandparents were married on October 8, 1938, and that to their reception they asked their guests to bring their own chairs because there wouldn't be enough for everyone. I hoped that these details I would never forget. Antonio turned the pages letting them crinkle and fall into place at will until there it was in front of us. Maria Micone, born Anna Maria Micone, married Michele Patavino in Montelongo on such and such a date becoming Anna Maria Patavino. Knowing her full name Anna Maria, not simply Maria was immediately important. I turned to my mom acknowledging in a different light, her full maiden name, Ann Marie Patavino. She had never known that she held the same name as her grandmother and I saw pride swell up in her as she recognized this. "That is my name," she said to Antonio. He took little interest in these details and continued to turn the pages. I was gathering evidence and facts, concrete numbers, in order to put them down on paper. But these moments truly belonged to my mother. For these were people to her, not just names and stories. They were the people she called Uncle and Grandma. I suppose she had always known and recognized that they were born in this country but in those times the past was something they tried to forget and push out of their consciousness. There was a silenced gap between the moments recorded on the papers in front of us, and my mother's life as an American that had been filled with the rumble of a new city, the talk of cars, and the prospect of tomorrow. However, I at this moment, felt that silence was becoming something audible as I watched my mother make sense of a history that no one talked about.

"I never knew her name was Anna Maria, not just Maria. I don't think Grandma and Grandpa knew either."

"Really, you think Grandpa never knew his own mother's full name."

"Oh, he probably knew, but just forgot." I felt sad for Grandpa knowing this. These are the details he needed to remember. That is why I was here.

"I wonder how much my uncles remembered of this place. They must have had some memories. I just wish I had heard them when I was young. I can't believe that this, Marco's house most likely, is where they were all born."

Friends of Antonio's walked through the room sporadically. They asked what we were doing and upon explanation found themselves momentarily interested in their own family history. But after five minutes of page turning, these long time residents of Montelongo lost interest. There is nothing romantic to them about this town, and about the people related to them. The fact that our relatives were born here and left for America did not impress them. Why should it? They left because their lives were hard, and remained hard until the day they died. For Antonio and his friends this record searching held no significance to an old man who sat at home watching the Yankee's spring training on TV. They wished Antonio farewell and were off to do whatever it is they do day-to-day in Montelongo. As he lit another cigarette, it became clear that Antonio has become committed to our search which has proven to be the most successful activity yet. We wonder if Pepino has intentionally withheld this visit in order to stretch out our stay as long as possible.

Why is it that we as Americans so longingly search for our roots? Is it because we are so displaced from our origins, that our traditions have been so manipulated and blended with others that they have lost their original meaning? Is it because our blood has been stretched so thin and far away from where it runs thickest that we have hardly anything to hold on to? And so we look, and we go back to that place to feel that at one point we belonged to something worth belonging to. I suppose with Grandpa on my mind, this is what I was doing. I went because he couldn't, but in doing this for him the time in Montelongo was becoming as much for my mom, and me, and my unborn kids. As a third generation American it is unusual to be a descendant of one country. Most of my peers are able to list off a number of places from which they hail, some of which they are not totally sure of. In all that I do, my Italian roots, and the traditions that have remained, have grounded me. The history we have translated into our present day life makes our family who we are. We eat 13 fish dishes on Christmas Eve, or try to, and pasta, or macaroni and "gravy", as we call it, takes precedence over turkey on Thanksgiving. We toast to La Familia. Desserts of sfuladele and ricotta pie are always served alongside Sambuca and espresso. We turn down the lights and nap at mid-day when we are together and practice with each other what we know of the language. As adults we share homes, never feeling the desire or need to be completely independent from each other. But I suppose for me, all this was not enough. I wanted to go as far back as I could and see where these traditions came from. To do this I had to go to Montelongo; it was like going back in time and as close as I was to get to the lives of my great grandparents. I needed to physically touch and observe the place and its people for myself, and let them seep into me as they had never been able to before in order to navigate my own past and future.

We woke to the sound of thunder undulating through the hills. The air had turned cool again. Neither winter nor spring had its hold on the village. Each tried to stake its claim but inevitably the other's force would be momentarily stronger until the roles were suddenly reversed, creating what we know to be the month of March. Hail was falling and winter was winning as I jumped from the bed and into warm clothes as quickly as possible. Outside the produce truck bounced ungracefully over the stone studded streets. "Fruta, verdura," the driver was shouting through the loud speaker to the sleeping houses as if its occupants didn't know what he was selling. The truck is the only clamor in town. My mom and I packed up returning each other's clothes and toiletries. I drove the two blocks to Lorenza's house, parked right in front, walked in the front door, and was offered a seat again in front of the fire. We took pictures and drank our last café. What can one say but grazie, to the three who had created the framework for a story that is still being told? We did not make promises of returning or open up invitations for them to visit us. We knew neither situation was likely. We drove away and it seemed like a different place than when we had arrived, anxious and unsure. We had gone from being Marco's house guests to the relatives of people who had spent their lives in this town. Though far from calling Montelongo home, we now had something, a piece of the past that was worth belonging to. But perhaps more so, we now had something that belonged to us, my mother and I. We had Marco, we had Pepino, we had the house, the hills, the quiet streets, lonesome church bells and we had the memory of experiencing these things together. We had come to understand our roots, one as a representative of the generation who, at one time, wanted to free herself from them, and the other from the generation who wanted more. In the process, the generation gap that separates my mother and me became for a time, almost invisible. We were strung together not by age, but by welcoming this town and its people into our vocabulary. We now had the same knowledge, gained from the same experiences that we would ultimately pass along to the generations that surrounded us at home. We did not speak until we had wound our way down that hilltop of stone and green. My mom having effortlessly endured days without hot water and clean sheets suddenly wanted, more than anything, a hot shower and a warm bed. I did not contest her desire nor her insistence on paying for a "nice" hotel and we drove north until she was satisfied. We slid our way through a small opening of the encapsulating bubble called Montelongo and remained unscathed but changed on the other side. We could look back, but from the outside the bubble had become opaque and we could no longer see in. And so we became tourists again speaking English and buying postcards, and I became again my mother's daughter. She treated me to dinner and hemmed my pants. Tomorrow I would take her to Pisa where she would fly, via London, back to Boston. We would be left to tell our stories on our own, but they would be missing something, until three months later when we could tell them together.

My mom and I have had our share of tearful good-byes, not because we didn't know when we'd see each other again, because it's never been that long, but because we'd miss each other until then. This goodbye was different. Yes, we'd miss each other until I returned home, but her getting on that plane in Pisa marked the end of a time in which secretly, we contemplated our past, laughed in the present, and strengthened our future. It was a time when we lived outside of time, outside of the realities that were our lives; it belonged to us. The experiences of Montelongo were tucked away in Marco's house, in the cemetery, in the olive trees that burned on the hillside, never to be had again. We were anxious to talk with home, but at the same time we were in no rush. For as soon as we began to translate into words our experiences they would lose the very thing that made them worth telling.

Leaving her in line to board the plane I walked slowly to the other end of the airport. Later she told me she watched me the whole way until I disappeared into the train station. I never turned around, but I knew she was watching me.

Christmas 2002

On a dark evening I walk into a camera shop in a deserted harbor village. I take my time deciding which picture frame to buy. It has to be perfect. I choose one, sleek and refined with room enough for five 4x6 photographs.

On the floor in front of the Christmas tree on Christmas Eve I select five pictures of Montelongo and place them carefully in the frame. The Micone farmhouse sits crystal clear in the center. With a black felt tipped pen I write as neatly as possible, Montelongo, Italy, at the bottom of the frame. I wrap the picture frame up in green and red paper and place on it a snowman tag on which I have written, "To: Grandpa From: Leigh." I was not thinking this would be his last Christmas.

Grandpa put great thought into hanging my gift, trying it in a number of locations, first in the bedroom, then above the fireplace, but nothing seemed right. On the far wall of the living room hung two individually framed photographs of Grandpa's parents. They had hung there, almost unnoticed, for years. Thoughtfully Grandpa took these down and placed them alongside the pictures of Montelongo. He hung all three frames in the front hallway of the house where everyone passed through and stalled for hellos and goodbyes.

"It looks real nice, Doll," he told me. "And now, every day when I walk by I say hello to my mom and dad, and you know, they were a real good looking pair!" The pictures of his parents were moved from a far wall to the front hall, and next to pictures of the village where they were born. In doing this Grandpa had moved this place and these people likewise to the front of his mind. I had helped bring them there. Every chance he had now Grandpa spoke to me in the Italian he thought he had long since forgotten. It was with the same thick accent I had heard in Montelongo. Somehow it had surfaced and he spoke with an ease that surprised us all. He was beginning to put all in place, preparing subconsciously for the days that would be his last. In the year and a half to follow, Grandpa and I were closer to each other than we'd ever been. I often took breaks from the loud bustle of my brother and cousins to spend quiet moments with Grandpa once the dinner table had long since been cleared. With each visit I made I brought him a box of his favorite pastries and with his full instruction I helped him mulch and plant his garden. Grandpa spoke to me often of Italy and asked me if I would like to live there. I told him yes, that it seemed as if at some point I would, and he was contented with this answer, even knowing that he would then be long gone. In these months I learned that knowing a grandparent in adulthood is a true blessing. They become more than Grandma or Grandpa in your mature mind. They become a fully realized person who has lived a long and meaningful life. I realized now how much of him I shared and that these shared qualities came not from daily interactions but from the same blood that ran through Grandpa and me. It is the same blood that runs through Montelongo.

July 16, 2003

It is Carmen Anthony's 92nd birthday. It is also the day he has decided to end his dialysis treatment. Until today he has continued to say, "It's not my time." Instead he waited until all the pieces fit together perfectly and chose for himself the very way in which he would pass on. The last days of his life were executed with precision and care, just as the decades that preceded them.

Grandpa sits quietly with my mom. He tells her what he wants for his birthday.

"No junk," he says. "I want a perennial garden on the side of the house with six red azaleas." He continues to explain to my mom running his soft fingers along the bed spread exactly how he wants it, and how it should be done.

"A scalloped edge coming in towards the center, the bushes four feet apart. In the fall I want to put a peony in the middle. I want Mom to be happy."

Grandpa lies in a hospital bed in his den. His wife, two daughters, son-in-law and all his grandchildren take turns holding his hand. At nightfall he wants to join the laughter coming from the living room and so slowly we help him make his way to his couch. He is surrounded by the family of his creation. We toast to him. A resounding "Salute" bounces off the wall and into the crevices of the high ceilings. And that is enough. Slowly he returns to his bed passing for the last time the pictures of Montelongo and his mother and father.

Thunder claps send warning of warm summer rain. I peel myself away from the couch that has nestled my body since mid-morning. In the other room my brother and cousins watch a movie all huddled like children on the living room floor.

"I'm going down to see Grandpa," I tell them.

"Dad, it's your one and only granddaughter," Aunt Emma says as I slide into the chair on the far side of his bed. He doses in and out of sleep as I sit quietly next to him looking through old photo albums of Grandpa and his handsome WWII days. He looks up at me and for a moment I look deep into his eyes and know his contentment. In less than an hour he is gone.

In the hot mid-day sun, my cousins and I break ground on the side of our grandparents' house. We turn topsoil, and laugh, and make sure the edge is perfect. We know that Grandpa is with us and we know we better get it right! We each, including my cousin's wife, plant one azalea bush and go inside to eat lunch with Grandma.

In my bedroom hangs an old picture of my family. Under it hangs a picture of my Grandpa. Under that hangs a picture of Montelongo. Each has grown out of the one that hangs beneath it. None can stand on its own. To their left, on a bedside table sits a picture of my mother and I on our latest trip to Mexico. We are tan and full of giggles happily sipping margaritas on the beach. Unintentionally, but not without significance this picture is set aside from the others. As much as we are both integral parts of our family's progression through time, my mother and I now have the ability to stand on our own.

December, 2003

About the Author

*A*NN VOTTA began her career as a junior high school English teacher in the mid-'60s. She moved on to consulting; first as an educational consultant and then as a nationally recognized work/life consultant. In between she served as a Professor of Education at several universities in the Boston area.  In 2000 she opened an antique and home décor business on Martha's Vineyard. Then her life changed dramatically in 2009 when she reunited with Alan. She is now focusing on memoir and travel writing and helping others as a life coach.

CPSIA information can be obtained at www.ICGtesting.com
Printed in the USA
LVOW05s1056020813

345755LV00005B/10/P